BURNING
QUESTIONS

MAL FLETCHER

BURNING

QUESTIONS

WORD PUBLISHING
Nelson Word Ltd
Milton Keynes, England

WORD AUSTRALIA
Kilsyth, Australia

NELSON WORD CANADA
Vancouver, B.C., Canada

STRUIK CHRISTIAN BOOKS (PTY) LTD
Cape Town, South Africa

JOINT DISTRIBUTORS SINGAPORE—
ALBY COMMERCIAL ENTERPRISES PTE LTD
and
CAMPUS CRUSADE, ASIA LTD

PHILIPPINE CAMPUS CRUSADE FOR CHRIST
Quezon City, Philippines

CHRISTIAN MARKETING NEW ZEALAND LTD
Havelock North, New Zealand

JENSCO LTD
Hong Kong

SALVATION BOOK CENTRE
Mal ysia

BURNING QUESTIONS

ISBN 1-86024-035-6

Unless otherwise stated, Scripture quotations are from the New International Version of the Bible, copyright 1973, 1978, 1984 by International Bible Society.

Those noted KJV are from the King James Version.

Those noted NCV are from the Holy Bible, New Century Version, copyright © 1987, 1988, 1991 by Word Publishing Ltd.

Those noted Barclays are from *The New Testament, A New Translation*, copyright © 1968, 1969 by William Barclay.

British Library in Cataloguing Data. A catalogue record for this book is available from the British Library.

Reproduced, printed and bound in Great Britain for Nelson Word Ltd. by Cox & Wyman Ltd., Reading.

95 96 97 98 / 10 9 8 7 6 5 4 3 2 1

Dear Miss Paige,

Thank you wherever you are.
When you first encouraged me to write a book
in your primary school grade 5 class,
I was apprehensive. But I had a go anyway.
It wasn't a great work of art (it certainly wasn't
very long), but I worked hard on it.
I'll never forget the feeling I had
when you read it to the class.
This is my third book (not counting my
5th grade effort), and I owe a lot to you
for making me think that writing was something (aside
from talking!) I could do. Thanks!

Mal Fletcher

Thanks to . . .

---

*Noël and Linda and all the team at
Nelson Word Ltd for your support.
Mike and Julie Smith for your
constant friendship.
Davina, greatest wife in the world,
and Deanna, Grant and Jade (Super Kids!)
I love you too much.
All of my great and radical friends
around the world!!*

CONTENTS

FOREWORD

A T THE EDGE OF THE next millennium, God is once again visiting the young across the world. Hundreds of teenagers and college students, no longer ashamed to identify with Jesus, are gathering openly to pray and proclaim the gospel in their schools and universities. Thousands more are already involved in some form of short-term or full-time Christian ministry each year. Tens of thousands at a time are gathering in auditoriums, stadiums and fields across the world to celebrate the transforming power of Christ and to share His love with others. Literally millions in the last few decades have turned in astonishing numbers to the Lordship of Christ.

Like Esther of old, in the midst of a dangerous and uncertain world, they feel they have 'come into the Kingdom for such a time as this'. Like four Hebrew boys in the days of Nebuchadnezzar, they have 'purposed not to defile themselves'. Like David about to face Goliath, they too can say in the face of giants David never dreamed of: '*Is there not a cause?*'

There are some who merely *watch* things happen, as the saying goes, and some who *make* things happen; the observers and the activists. But every now and then you come across a man with the unique ability to do both; he who both sees with a prophet's eye what is going on in a world and has the giftings to affect it with power.

Mal Fletcher is one of these men. Already an icon in his home nation of Australia, Mal and some of his talented team-mates under God have spearheaded some of the most effective and innovative ministry outreaches to the young in the contemporary history of his nation. He is a thinker, an artist, a life-long student of the ever-changing youth culture of the Western world, and above all a man who loves God and loves young people. He has written for his ministry before and written for his country. Now he is writing for the world. This practical, insightful and wide-ranging book is exactly the kind of work we need now to help challenge and equip the young army of Christ rising for righteousness across the world.

I commend both him and his gift to you as a book of significant questions that point without cant, cloud or compromise to our only real Answer.

Winkie Pratney, January 1995

1

LOST IN THE FOREST

– LEARNING TO SEE THE WORLD RIGHT SIDE UP –

. . . We grabbed the guy, tied his hands and feet and threw him into the boot of the car. We'd blindfolded him, of course, and stuffed cotton wool in his ears. There was no way he'd ever be able to tell where we were taking him.

We drove to a forest about a hundred miles away, found the darkest spot we could and stopped the engine. We took him out of the boot. He was shivering with cold and mumbling about having bad cramps in his arms and legs.

When we last saw him he was staring blankly into space, a look of utter confusion on his face. He had no compass or map, and there were no signposts for miles. If he ever found his way out of that forest, it'd be a miracle!

HAVE YOU EVER felt just a little lost in the big wide world? Like you've been kidnapped, dragged a long way from home, dumped in a forest, and left to find your own way back—without a map? Like someone's taken you for a drive down the information super-highway, but forgotten to give you a compass so you can make sense of all the changes around you?

You have? So have I, my friend. And we're not alone.

Which way is up?

Twenty years ago a man called Alvin Toffler was warning the world about what he called the 'roaring current of change'. He prophesied that, as technological progress rolled on at an ever greater pace, it would carry many people away from their sense of security. Rapid change, he said, would leave people feeling increasingly disorientated and bewildered.

Today, a whole generation can testify to the accuracy of Toffler's predictions. We're facing issues which our parents' generation did not. New technologies have made things possible which were never dreamt of before. Life is easier in many ways, but it can also be far more complicated and unsettling, because of the multitude of choices we find ourselves facing. For some of us, *the only certainty is change itself!*

What's the answer to our confusion? Is it 'less science', or 'fewer gadgets'? No, most of us know that's not it. The problem goes deeper than that. Somewhere, somehow, we've lost our moral compass, our inner sense of direction and security. We've become a society where everyone knows the cost of something, but no one can tell you the value of anything!

Where can we find value systems that work?

Some of us think nostalgia is the answer, a return to simpler, more innocent times. Maybe the fifties were the 'Happy Days' we see on TV. Perhaps the *Beverley Hillbillies*, in all their naïveté, knew something we don't! And so the fads come and go: a yearning for the sixties, then for the seventies, then for the fifties again. But escapism doesn't last, and the past is seldom what we think it was.

So some of us turn to 'alternative spirituality'. We buy the best-selling ramblings of New Age gurus to help us get in touch with our 'inner guide'. We know that there's more to life than meets the eye—we certainly hope there is!—so we resonate with films like *Ghost*, *Leap of Faith*, and even *Angels in the Outfield*. Our hearts tell us that we need some kind of help from above if we're ever going to make it through the moral maze we're living in.

Some of us just give up, and stop thinking altogether, preferring to party on and let things run as they will. Bono of U2 sings, 'You miss too much these days if you stop to think . . . '[1]

But there are others who, in the midst of the searching, eventually realise what it is that's *really* missing. Why are we confused in this high-tech world? Why does all our material affluence still leave us feeling alone and lost?

It's because we've taken God out of the frame. We're trying to make sense of God's world without reference to His nature, which is the pattern upon which the whole universe was built. We're like photographers trying to take pictures while standing on shifting sands. We have nothing solid under our feet, so our view of things is blurred.

When we never stop to ask, 'What would God want in this situation, or with this issue?', we're throwing away our moral compass. We're leaving ourselves (and the next generation) in a dark forest, without any point of reference to help us get home safely.

There IS something out there (thank God!)

In a world where things and people change all the time, God is the only One who doesn't change—*ever!* He doesn't just *act* truly, He *is* absolute Truth. He doesn't just *behave* fairly, He *is* Justice itself. He doesn't just *feel* love, He *is* Love! Take God out of your world and you're removing all these good things and more. You're creating a 'moral black hole' that sucks all hope into itself and leaves people in confusion.

'When a man stops believing in God,' said a very wise man, 'he doesn't believe in nothing, he believes in anything!' When God doesn't figure in your search for truth, or when you assume that human beings are the highest reference for morals, you'll be a sucker for any old philosophy that comes along.

That's what this book is about—*putting God back in the frame where the really big questions are concerned.*

I want you to take a look with me at some of the major moral and human rights issues of our time and see if we can't figure out basically which way is up and which is down. We won't be basing our judgements on what's convenient, or what 'feels' right. We'll be asking the question: if God is as the Bible describes Him, how would He respond when faced with this situation or issue?

Through the centuries, since the time of Christ, there have been hundreds of people who have asked that very question. The answers they found gave them the wisdom and the strength to stand against the status quo and change history for the better. You may think all Christians are invaders from the planet *Nerd* who've come to bore everyone into submission. It may seem like most Bible-believing people are only into meaningless 'Christian punctuation', (you know, 'praise the Lord anyway', that kind of thing.) Take a good long look at history, though, and you'll find a *very* different story!

John Wesley was a man of great character, courage and conviction. He thought deeply about the world he lived in, and responded to the needs of his age with such passion that many historians credit him with having saved England from civil war and revolution. He was the man they say 'restored to a nation its soul'.[2]

George Fox, a Quaker radical, spent long periods of time in prison for taking a brave stand against slavery, which was a popular part of 'respectable' society in his time. William Wilberforce not only stood against the evil trade in African slaves; he was also a founding member of the RSPCA—a man ahead of his time!

William Booth, with his wife Catherine, took the Christian message and good works to the streets of poverty-stricken London. Today, the Salvation Army, which they formed, is one of the world's most respected charities.

George Muller responded to the plight of homeless children by setting up some of Europe's first orphanages. Horatio Spafford and his wife, originally from Chicago, rescued many young Arab girls who had been abandoned by their parents in the Palestine of the 1800s.

In the young nation of America, another group of preacher-activists arose to challenge the way things were and point the way to a better society in God's name. One of these awesome figures, Charles Finney, said that, 'The great business of the church is to reform the world. The church of Christ was originally organised to be a body of reformers.'[3] He certainly lived up to that belief!

How many others could we cite here? Martin Luther King boldly proclaimed his dream of little white boys and little black boys holding hands together in peace. It cost him his life. Mother Teresa left a comfortable career as a teacher in a middle-class school to devote her life to the poorest of the poor in down-town Calcutta.

All of these truly great people—and hundreds of others—were motivated by one thing above all else: *a profound understanding of the heart of God*. They knew Him as the One who stands up for the oppressed, the One who loves the unlovely, the One who brings hope where despair has reigned.

So, if *you* are ready to think about the world you live in and to change it for the better; if *you* want to find a solid footing for the choices you make; if *you* want to help others find the moral compass and step out of the forest . . . *read on!*

REFERENCES:

1. U2, 'Until The End Of The World', *Achtung Baby* (Island Records, 1991).
2. John Wesley Bready, quoted by John Stott, *Issues Facing Christians Today* (Marshall Pickering, 1984), p.3.
3. Ibid., p.5.

STUDY GUIDE

Extensive university research and tests involving small mice have now revealed that change is here to stay—the world will continue to change.

Professor Claudius Fritzenbacher III
Emeritus Professor,
Dept. of Verifiable Myths, Camford University.

Warm-ups

List some of the major changes which have occurred in the world over the past twenty-five years or so. In your opinion, which two or three have had the biggest impact on the lives of people in your country (for good or evil?) Why have these changes affected people in the way they have?

Alvin Toffler believed that rapid change would cause many people to feel confused about their world. How can people be equipped to better handle change?

Study/Discussion

Read Ezekiel 39:7 and Psalm 89:14. What do you think is meant by each of the terms used to describe God here?

Read 1 John 4:8–10; Psalm 145:9,15; James 5:11 and Ephesians 1:6. List the qualities of God's nature described in these passages. In your own words, what does each of these terms mean?

Read 1 John 5:20 and 1 Corinthians 1:9. What does it mean to say that God is 'true' and 'faithful'? (See also Joshua 21:45.)

Read Leviticus 11:45. Knowing what we do about God's nature, how does He expect us to respond?

Getting Started
In the light of the above qualities of God's nature, what are some of the specific changes you think God would like made in your city and country—how could God's nature be better expressed where you live?

What changes/improvements can you make in your own life to better imitate these qualities?

Further Resources
Alvin, Toffler, *Future Shock* (Pan Books, 1971).

Tom, Sine, *Wild Hope* (Monarch, 1991).

George, Barna, *The Frog in the Kettle* (Regal Books, 1990).

T. C. Hammond and D. F. Wright, *In Understanding Be Men*, chapters 1 and 2 (IVP, 1968).

2

ARE THERE TEARS IN HEAVEN?

– WHY DO GOOD PEOPLE SUFFER? –

*It was April 1994. I was in Denmark. What I saw
moved me. The 7 o'clock BBC news was beaming into
my room the picture of a little boy—he couldn't have
been more than seven years old—who had just lost an
eye in a mortar attack in the fierce ethnic fighting in
Sarajevo. 'I was resting,' he mumbled through an inter-
preter, 'and I saw blood falling on my hand, from my
eye. Now I am afraid.'*

*I have a son his age and I felt angry for this boy. Why
do the innocent suffer so much in this world's conflicts?*

THE UN REPORTS that there are 200,000 children
under fifteen years of age who are involved in real
wars the world over. Some boys of twelve are chasing snipers when they should be chasing girls! As I write
this, the radio beside me is telling me that on any given day
100,000 kids in good ol' US of A take guns to school.

Poverty is a normal way of life for 800 million people
in the world today—they earn less than £61 per year.
Malnutrition kills an estimated 40,000 children every
day and in some developing countries children are sold by
poor parents for as little as £25–£40.

War is a game too many want to play—at least fifteen nations have an A-bomb and twenty-five are trying to get one to keep up with the Joneses. Even in this age of scaling back nuclear arsenals, we still live in a spaceship which is armed with enough power to self-destruct many times over.

When you watch the news one question seems to throb inside your head—*why?* Oh sure, there are always cruel monsters in this world who deserve everything they get, but when it comes to the mostly innocent majority: *why?* Is God playing some huge joke on us or does He get His kicks from watching us squirm?

The centre of the Bible is not the middle page!

'But I don't believe in a God,' some will say. Well, I pity them. Sorry, but I do. I can't think of anything more despairing than choosing to believe that what we see is all there is. That we are all meaningless little blobs of matter in an absurd, chaotic universe. That the best any of us can do is make up our own little meaning for this thing called life. That the only God there is, is the one we invent for ourselves, or the one who lies dormant within us. (Man, if I'm God we're all in a fat lot of trouble!)

If you've completely given up on God, you've pretty much given up hope. The best you can do is close your weary eyes and sing along with Steve Taylor:

Life unwinds like a cheap sweater
But since I gave up hope I feel a lot better

And the truth gets blurred like a wet letter
But since I gave up hope I feel a lot better![1]

Believing in something beyond ourselves is important, but it's not enough to know that you 'sort of, maybe, perhaps' believe in some vague notion of a Supreme Being. It's vital to evaluate exactly what *kind* of God you're prepared to believe in. Your concept of God's nature will shape your whole view of our world and its joys and pain. There are basically four options you have open to you:

1. The God of Star Wars

This one really took off in the West during the psychedelic 60s as people looked to the east and Hinduism and Buddhism for spiritual inspiration. It was helped along by movies about *The Force* being 'with you' in the seventies and has found wider acceptance in the New Age eighties and nineties.

You wouldn't invite this god to your party—he has no personality! No, I don't just mean he has no sense of humour. He—or should 'he' be 'it' in this case?—doesn't possess any of the attributes of personality, or personhood, such as will. God is a force, a mystic spook-thing which somehow manages to be everywhere in everything, but can't bring itself to feel anything, because only persons have feelings. There's no sense praying to this god—the phone's off the hook.

2. The God of Father Mulcahy

Do you remember *M*A*S*H*, the long-running TV series? Father Mulcahy was the friendly neighbourhood priest on camp. He was a lovable enough guy with a warm smile who tried, in the horrors of war, to offer sympathy and a kind word to both patients and medicos based at Mobile Army Surgical Hospital no. 4077.

Mulcahy was a real nice guy, sure. But you wouldn't call him the hero of the series. He cared until his clerical pores bled, but he was often found wanting in the practical know-how department. When people needed a little dose of old-fashioned niceness in their lives he was definitely their man. But when they required down-to-earth, pragmatic ideas they could actually *use* in their daily struggles, they were better off relying on the cunning, though flawed, Hawkeye Pierce.

Mulcahy represents a god who often wears a concerned look and even feels deeply about the pain we go through, but has no power to do anything for us. The best we can hope for are a few platitudes about there being a silver lining in every cloud. A nice guy, but no help in a crisis.

3. The God of Saddam Hussein
This god's the mother of all misery-mongers. He's heavy handed and harsh, but very convenient for war-merchants like our man in Iraq. If you're in his employ you're involved in a holy war, a *literal* war, against all infidels. This god isn't smart or subtle enough to win people over to his way of thinking through gentle persuasion, he must use the sledgehammer approach to bring change. He is all powerful but has no compassion—or not so much that you'd notice.

4. The God of a Cross and an Empty Tomb
This is your fourth alternative—the God of biblical Christianity.

I think I can hear a few murmurs of discontent at this point. Some people will object to my making a distinction between the Christian God and the deities of other major religions. They'll ask questions like, 'Doesn't the Bible also say that God is "Spirit" and "all-present"?' And, 'Isn't the Christian God also supposed to be very caring?' Or, 'Didn't the Old Testament also get a little blood-thirsty at times?' So where's the difference?

If I told you I could fly, you'd send me to a doctor who has a couch and get some coloured pills! But if I told you the same thing while standing in front of a Jumbo jet, you'd accept every word. Why? Because the context, the backdrop, affects your perception of what I'm saying. Without the jet in the background, you have no way of understanding what I mean.

There are two things which form the centre of Christianity: the cross on which Jesus went to His death, and the empty tomb He left behind when He rose from the dead. Unless you're willing to keep the cross and the resurrection always in mind, you can never really hear what the Bible is telling you about God. Without them the whole picture is out of focus, it makes no sense. Those two historical events reveal certain key things about God.

Firstly, that He is a person, not simply a 'force'. Yes, the Bible does say that He is in essence a 'Spirit' (John 4:24)—He does not have a body made up of molecules as we do. But the cross and resurrection show the characteristics of His personhood, especially His immense love, His sense of justice and His unfailing hope for humanity.

When was the last time you saw people wearing little golden electric chairs or hangman's nooses around their necks as jewellery? You've never seen it? No, of course not.

But people *do* wear crosses! Yet all three objects were designed for the one purpose—to execute serious criminals. In fact, of the three, many who have studied the effects of crucifixion would call it the worst, the most inhumane, of the three ways to die. Jesus took a symbol of hatred, despair and incredible cruelty and turned it into a symbol of love, hope and mercy!

According to the Bible God's greatest act in our history was one of profound love. Before time began, God the Father made a decision, in love, that He would send His Son to die for the failures of the human race (John 3:16). This is not some schmaltzy TV sitcom love, but a strong and enduring compassion. Mindless spooks don't make decisions and they don't love, because they don't possess will.

The cross also reveals the justice in God's nature. The fact that God loves so greatly doesn't mean that He'll go lightly on evil. He is compassionate *and* He is just. What kind of universe would we be living in if there were no fundamental integrity, no 'rightness' at its core? Jesus always claimed that He would take the punishment which should have fallen on us (Matthew 20:28). His death, He said, would remove God's anger from our lives.

When Jesus went to the cross at Golgotha, His self-sacrifice satisfied at the same time both God's justice *and* God's undying love for humanity. The resurrection shows us that God accepted that sacrifice—*and* that He wants to work miracles in *our* lives (Acts 10:37–44; John 14:12).

To answer the final objection: yes, the Old Testament does describe some fairly gruesome wars fought in the name of God. In this fractured and morally fallen world God has sometimes allowed certain things to be done which were not what He really intended when He created it. That's partly because He has invested in us the ability to make morally binding choices. To have allowed us anything less would have been to create robotoids instead of people. God couldn't give us the power of choice without facing the risk that we might abuse it.

But sometimes in pre-Christian times, God intervened in history to save humanity from itself! Think about it: if He hadn't acted at different times to hold back the ambitions of megalomaniacs, the world wouldn't have lasted long enough for there to have been any Jesus, any cross, any salvation. Whenever God has intervened in history with anger, His intention was to preserve us, to stop the rot before we could destroy ourselves and our world— to keep us from a potentially worse fate at our own hands. The God of the Bible has never disciplined out of some kind of twisted, sadistic pleasure ('These guys annoy me, let's nuke 'em!'). His attitude has been something like: 'We'd better do something firm to save these guys, before there's nothing left to save.'

Here's how Jeremiah the Bible prophet saw God's discipline: 'For men are not cast off by the Lord for ever. Though he brings grief, he will show compassion, so great is his unfailing love. For he does not willingly bring affliction or grief to the children of men' (Lamentations 3:31–33).

Hosea, another prophetic voice, called to his nation, 'Come, let us return to the Lord. He has torn us to pieces but he will heal us; he has injured us but he will bind up our wounds' (Hosea 6:1). Whenever Israel had broken its love agreement, or covenant, with God, He would send a prophet like Hosea to warn them to turn. If they still

27

wouldn't listen, He used events, even wars—as a last resort—to correct them (Hosea 6:2–7). But in Hosea, and throughout the Bible, the emphasis is always on God's restoration of those He has had to discipline. Even Gentile nations are promised a part in God's great new kingdom (Acts 11:1–18; Romans 15:8–12). That's the heart of a Father, not a tyrant!

Everything you ever wanted to know about God (but were afraid to ask!)

In Bible terms, God's great goal through all those pre-Christian times, when His patience was sometimes stretched to the limit, was to bring Christ onto the scene to save humankind. According to the Bible, everything there is to know about the character of God was to be found in the person of Jesus (Colossians 2:9).

Someone put it like this, 'Jesus is God saying, "This is what I'm like." ' Jesus Himself said, 'Anyone who has seen me has seen the Father' (John 14:9). He claimed to be one with God and doing God's work (John 10:30; 8:28–29). If you look at the man Jesus, what you see is God talking and walking like us, making Himself understandable to us. Jesus sums up everything you ever wanted to know about God.

But isn't Jesus just an invention; a convenient myth for religious people to lean on? You could be excused for thinking like that if the Bible was the only record of Jesus' existence. But it's not. F. F. Bruce wrote this: 'Some writers may toy with the fancy of a "Christ-myth", but they do not do so on the ground of historical evidence . . . It is not historians who propagate the "Christ-myth" theories.'[2]

That's because historians know there are many early sources outside of the Bible which speak about a real man called Jesus of Nazareth. Those sources are not all friendly to Him either! Ancient writers such as Flavius Josephus, Lucian of Samosata and Seutonias, a court official under Hadrian, all make direct references to a real Jesus, and the church He started, in their work.[3] None of them were Christian believers.

Thallus, a Samaritan-born historian also speaks about Jesus and the time of His death, as does Phlegun, another first-century history writer. Even the Jewish Talmuds refer to the existence of Jesus of Nazareth, who was crucified 'on the eve of Passover'.[4] They don't speak of Jesus in very favourable terms, and that fact alone shows us that they're not out to do the Christians any favours by supporting any 'Jesus myths'.

So what was Jesus like? By far the most material we have on Jesus is found in four different historical records which we now call the 'Gospels'. These were written by four of Jesus' close followers—or people who knew them very well—between AD 40 and 100. The authors are very different men, who each write in their own style.

But are the Gospels we have today, the same as these early copies, or have they been distorted by translators and scribes with ulterior motives? Our copies of the Gospels line up with the earliest copies in a startling way. Homer, a blind minstrel and poet of ancient Greece, wrote an epic poem which he called the *Iliad*. It's a story about a section of the Trojan War and is regarded as an ancient masterpiece. Very few copies of this work which date back to the time of its creation exist. The earliest copies date from around 400 BC—at least 300 years after it was written. Yet nobody questions that the

Iliad we have today is pretty much as the author wrote it.

For the New Testament, however, scholars have discovered over 24,000 early manuscripts, in several languages. The earliest copies we have date back to AD 125 —that's only twenty-five years after the last Gospel was written! No other ancient writings have anywhere near as much material to support their reliability.[5]

The *Iliad* has 15,600 lines. There are 764 lines which scholars say are doubtful—no one is sure that they were part of the original. The New Testament, on the other hand, has 20,000 lines, of which only forty have been in question![6]

So, what was the Jesus of the Gospels like? He certainly wasn't some passionless robotoid who couldn't care less what human beings do to one another. He knew how to cry *and* how to let His compassion move Him to action (Matthew 9:36). He could get angry too—man, could He!—but it was *only ever* an anger motivated by a righteous passion to stand up for the helpless and abused (Matthew 23:1–4).

As a leader He led from the front—He always gave out more commitment than He received in return. He taught us to live the same way, going the extra mile in meeting each other's needs (Matthew 5:41). He showed that real influence comes through servanthood (Mark 10:44). That's the kind of God the Bible is on about.

Unfortunately, the various gods of Skywalker, Mulcahy and Hussein are each based upon caricatures of the truth. When you remove Jesus, the cross and the empty tomb out of the frame, you get a very distorted picture of what God is like.

What on earth is God playing at?

OK, so if God did come to Earth in human form, you wouldn't expect Him to ever ask the 'why?' question, would you? I mean, He ought to know all the answers and be above all this suffering and uncertainty! Actually, when you read the Gospels you will find that Jesus knew a great deal about suffering, and that even He asked 'why?'

You won't read about crosses as a means of execution these days. I mean, newspapers don't carry banner headlines which say, 'Fifty Scumbags Crucified Today!' But that's what you might have seen if you'd lived in the glorious, and incredibly cruel, Roman Empire.

I've been to Israel on two occasions. I've seen the kinds of crosses the Romans liked to hang people on—chilling is the only word I can find to describe the feeling.

Here's how one scholar described death by crucifixion: 'The unnatural position made every movement painful; the lacerated veins and crushed tendons throbbed with incessant anguish; the wounds . . . gradually gangrened; the arteries—especially at the head and the stomach—became swollen . . . [and, besides all this] there was the intolerable pang of a burning and raging thirst; and all these physical complications caused an internal excitement and anxiety, which made the prospect of death itself . . . bear the aspect of delicious and exquisite release.'[7] *Not* a nice way to die!

By the time Jesus was crucified, He had already suffered enough to make most men crumble. He had been whipped with a Roman *flagrum*—a nice little instrument made of strands of leather with pieces of bone tied in at the ends. He had been assaulted and spat upon by soldiers. He had a mocking crown made of huge thorns pushed down on His head. And He had been dragged across town all night from one courtroom to another, as they tried to work out what they were going to do with Him. They had made Him carry His own cross out of town to the hill called Golgotha ('place of the skull') and then He had huge Roman spikes driven through His hands and feet (John 18–19; Luke 23).

This man knew something about suffering! It was while He looked down from the cross that Jesus asked this heart-rending question, 'My God, My God, why have you for-saken me?' (Matthew 27:46) Notice the magic word here? Yes, 'why'. God's own Son asked the big one!

Hey, asking the 'why?' question is not wrong as far as God is concerned. Oh, so you thought He would be offended? No, He has no problem with you wondering why things are the way they are at times. But please note: when Jesus asked this question, He did it with a certain kind of attitude. The way He asked it and the way I do, are different in at least three ways.

Jesus was not part of the problem

A young woman asked me why she had been through three miscarriages. I thought through all my years of Bible reading and sermon-tasting and I couldn't think of one cliché that would do the trick. I was lost for words (unusual for me).

Thankfully the words of the late Francis Schaeffer came to the rescue. Many young people would write to Schaeffer and ask him what they should do about difficult situations in their lives. He would often remind them that, 'in the midst of this fallen world things are abnormal; they have been changed from that which God had made originally.'[8] Unfair things happen in this fallen world.

Humankind was God's wonderful, deliberate choice—there were no mistakes. God didn't set out to create man and say, 'Oops, I've made a monkey by mistake . . . Oh well, give it a few million years and it'll turn into a man anyway!' You are *not* a cosmic accident! But in so many ways this world is not the way God designed it to be. So much of it has been flawed by human selfishness, greed and shortsightedness. Much of human suffering is the fault not of God, but of humanity!

Let's face it—often we can't live up to our own standards, let alone God's. Even in the high-tech, whizz-bang modern age we're prone to be an odd mixture of iron and clay, gold and dust. We design hospitals, then fill them with victims of our own wars.

Years ago, *Time* magazine ran a series of articles under the title *What's Wrong With the World?* G. K. Chesterton, a writer and committed Christian, addressed a letter to the editor. It said: 'Sir, in answer to your articles titled "What's Wrong With the World?" . . . I am!' Here's how Bruce Springsteen expressed it in a song called *Two Faces Have I*:

I met a girl and we ran away
I swore I'd make her happy every day
And how I made her cry
Two faces have I
Sometimes mister I feel sunny and wild
Lord I love to see my baby smile
Then dark clouds come rolling by
Two faces have I

One that laughs one that cries
One says hello one says goodbye
One does things I don't understand
Makes me feel like half a man . . . [9]

I want to do the right thing, says Springsteen, but, well, it seems to elude me! (By the way, you'll find some very similar sentiments expressed by Paul in the Bible: Romans 7:15–20.)

Have you ever read Hans Christian Anderson's immortal tale *The Emperor's New Clothes?* Most of us, at some time or other, are like the vain, pompous king in this story. We kid ourselves. This king paid a couple of would-be tailors (read 'conmen') to make him a special suit. The tricksters told him they were weaving with a magic thread which was so special that only the very wise and noble in his kingdom would be able to see it. The king and all his courtiers, not wanting to appear stupid, admired the work of these rip-off merchants, 'ooh-ing' and 'aah-ing' at what was really nothing at all!

Finally, the king wanted to show off by wearing his new suit in the big parade. Only one little boy in the crowd was willing to say what he really saw—a naked king! The crowd began to laugh, and that's when it finally hit the king—he *was* naked, there *was* no suit of clothes. Too proud and vain to admit his folly, he carried on with the parade, as he was! But something *was* missing.

Like that king, we enjoy telling ourselves how good we look, clothed in our own virtue and righteous thoughts. Then one day something happens which reminds us of how vulnerable and flawed we really are. We talk ourselves into feeling secure, then some event or unkind word blows our confidence out of the water. What's *really* sad is that we often carry on regardless, too proud to admit our frailty.

According to the Bible, we were created in the image of God and so are capable of noble and selfless works. At the same time we are marred by our failure to submit to God's rule. With great capacity for good, we live with a twist in our nature toward evil.

Mal, are you saying that I'm personally to blame for every bad thing which has ever happened to me? Was the little boy in Sarajevo guilty of some crime? Did the young woman bring on herself the miscarriages she suffered? Or did the Jews deserve the Holocaust, or the South Africans the apartheid system?

No. Even Jesus taught that this kind of thinking is wrong (John 9:3). People sometimes get what they *don't* deserve in this fallen world. It's just that, because of our 'bent' inner nature, *we are part of the problem, not the solution.* So the 'Why?' question could be turned around like this: 'Why *Not* !?' I mean, maybe you and I *have* brought some of this on ourselves.

Jesus was pure of all sin—He did not share the twisted part of our nature (Hebrews 4:15). If any man deserved better treatment than He got, it was Jesus Christ! Yet He endured it. Why? To become our 'fall guy' or our 'stand-in', to give us a whole new quality of life (Romans 6:23, 2 Corinthians 5:14–15).

Jesus didn't question God's integrity

Here's another major difference between the 'why?' question when I ask it, and the same question when God's Son asked it. For Jesus, it was a cry of intense sorrow; for me it is more often dominated by self-justification, self-pity, anger at God and doubt as to His loyalty (or His sanity!).

In the Bible there is a very clear line drawn between 'testing God' and 'putting God to the test' (see Malachi 3:10, Matthew 4:7). What's the difference? To 'put God to the test' is to question His integrity. It's shaking the fist at Him and shouting: 'Go on, God . . . do something . . . You can't, can You? . . . You're not even listening, are You?! *How dare You do this to me*!' There's nothing but self-right- eous smugness in that. I'm just wanting to show what God *can't* do! I'm provoking Him (a dangerous pastime!).

To 'test' God is to look forward to His response, to want to prove, or display His goodness through my situa- tion. I want Him to show what He *can* do in my problem, because I love Him and have faith in His good character. I believe that's the kind of attitude in Jesus' heart when He asked the 'why?' question. His wasn't a cry of bitterness or rage *against* God, but of empathy *with* God!

Let me explain that statement this way. A preacher I know tells of an intense experience he went through while praying in the Garden of Gethsemane, just outside Jerusalem. This is the place where Jesus spent His final hours as a free man.

My friend asked God to give him a small taste of what Jesus went through in those final minutes before He was handed over to His enemies. What happened next stunned and shocked him. He felt as if a film was playing inside his head. It was rated triple 'X'! He was watching some of the most gruesome murders ever committed throughout his- tory. He saw the aftermath of some of humanity's most bloodthirsty wars. Then the eyes of his imagination watched in horror as women were raped, children were beaten and men tortured. He knew that each event was repeated thousands, perhaps millions of times throughout man's reign on earth.

All this lasted only a very short time, but the effect was intense enough to leave him weeping and in deep anguish of spirit. How could God's world have come to this?

As this imagined film, this vision, came to an end my friend thought he heard a silent whisper: 'That's just a *small* part of what My Son took upon Himself in this Garden. What you feel is *minute* compared to His agony of spirit!'

When you look at human history like this, from God's point of view, you're not asking, 'Where is God?' but *'Where on earth is man?'* When Jesus cried, 'Why?' I think He felt more intensely than you or I ever could the agony of our separation from God. If He was angry with anything, it was with death itself, which was never part of God's original design for His earth.

As Francis Schaeffer put it, 'It is proper to be angry in the midst of this fallen world, but you must be careful to be angry at the right person . . . Jesus, who claimed to be God, was angry when He stood before the tomb of Lazarus— without being angry with Himself.'[10]

But notice, Jesus' 'why?' question is addressed to 'My God'. In Jesus' broken heart God is still God. He is still to be revered and honoured as God. What's more, He's still 'my' God. Jesus was not disillusioned with God, He still gave allegiance to Him, knowing that He can make light shine out of even the blackest night (Romans 8:28–30).

In one of Matthew Henry's great commentaries on the Bible, he makes this bold statement, 'If we want the faith of assurance, we must live by the faith of adherence.' If we want the constant security of knowing that God is with us, we must be willing to stick with Him even through the tough times. Jesus *had* the faith of adherence!

Jesus wasn't 'Just Singing the Blues!'

I took my children to see an English cathedral not so long ago. My son, who was seven, walked along beside the pews looking at their wooden book rails. 'Hey dad,' he said, in a not-so-quiet whisper, 'it's really cool that they have so many Bibles to use.'

'Actually son,' I replied, 'they're prayer books.'

'Why do people need books to help them to pray?'

A fair question, I guess. Most prayer is (or should be) just as natural as talking to a friend. You do not need books for that (unless you have incredibly formal friends!). There are times and situations, however, when I've found I just do not know what to pray for. I could do with some help from someone who has already been down this path before.

That's when prayer books aren't such a dumb idea—they can help to get you started on what to pray. (But you must make sure they're only your servant, never your master, or your prayer times will feel like chewing chunky wet cement!) When Jesus asked the 'why?' question, He was actually reciting part of a prayer King David had written hundreds of years before. It's found in Psalm 22.

The Psalms are the Bible's hit parade—the top 150 chart-stoppers of ancient Israel. Fifty-seven of these are songs of lament. Just over one third of the Bible's famous songs express some sort of sorrow or pain. *God knows how to sing the blues!* I don't know what music it was played to, but

I can imagine Psalm 22 starting in a minor key. The first half is a cry of pain. Here are a few of the lyrics:

> My God, my God, why have you forsaken me?
>> Why are you so far from saving me,
>> so far from the words of my groaning?
> O my God, I cry out by day, but you do not answer,
>> by night, and am not silent . . .
> But I am a worm and not a man,
>> scorned by men and despised by the people.
> All who see me mock me;
>> they hurl insults, shaking their heads:
> 'He trusts in the LORD;
>> let the LORD rescue him.
> Let him deliver him,
>> since he delights in him . . .'
> Do not be far from me,
>> for trouble is near
>> and there is no one to help.

And so it goes. So far it could be Muddy Waters singing to a blues riff. But the mood changes; the chart might have switched to a more joyful major key. The end of the Psalm is a jubilant cry of hope:

> The poor will eat and be satisfied;
>> they who seek the LORD will praise him—
>> may your hearts live for ever!
> All the ends of the earth
>> will remember and turn to the LORD,
> and all the families of the nations will
>> bow down before him,
> for dominion belongs to the LORD
>> and he rules over the nations . . .

Posterity will serve him;
   future generations will be told about the Lord.
They will proclaim his righteousness
   to a people yet unborn—
   for he has done it.

Yes, God comes to the rescue! In the midst of crucifix-ion, Jesus was quoting a song which started in pain and ended in hope. Sure, He only quoted the first verse, but He certainly would have been familiar with the rest.

Always look on 'The Bright Side of Life?'

Some people will tell you that when Jesus hung on the cross He became aware, for the first time, that His preten-sions to being God's Son were nothing more than delusions of grandeur. Suddenly, they'll say, He came to the shocking conclusion that He had totally deluded Himself. Knowing this, He sank into despair and died, perhaps the world's saddest man.

But the historical record paints a completely different picture. As His strength ebbed away, Jesus sounded any-thing but despairing. In agony, yes. Lonely, yes. Heart-broken by man's folly and His own present suffering, perhaps. But in despair of the future? *Definitely not.*

For three years His friends and disciples followed Him around the countryside, and on many occasions they heard Him talk about His own death—though they didn't always understand what He was saying at the time (John 5:24–28). He even knew *how* He was going to die, weeks before it happened (John 12:32). At His final meal with His followers, He told them to share a dinner like this often, so they could remember Him when He had gone (Luke 22:19). They had absolutely no idea what He was on about!

He had also foretold many times that He was going to return from the dead. Even at the beginning of His public life He was teaching on the resurrection (John 2:18–22). He also told people that, after His death, He would return to His Father in heaven where He would once more take up His former glory (John 13:30–33)! And when His enemies finally came to arrest Him late one night—a spineless bunch they were—where was He? Hiding in a corner somewhere? No, He went boldly out to face them. 'Who is it you want?' He asked (John 18:4). These are not the words and actions of a man who is confused about or running from His fate.

On the cross He said to one of the thieves crucified with Him, 'Today you will be with me in paradise' (Luke 23:43). He promised this unfortunate chap a place in heaven! Does He sound bewildered to you? Near the end, as the last of His strength slipped away, He cried out to God, 'It is finished' (John 19:30). Notice, it's not, '*I* am finished!' This is a cry of victory—He is saying, 'The dream is fulfilled, the work is done!'

These are all words of hope. As it turns out, His faith in the future is well founded. Three days after dying, He is again making personal appearances among His followers, risen victorious over death itself. He has died *and* lived to tell the tale!

All you need is . . . hope!

There are three qualities which will always exist in God's universe—no matter how bleak the weather gets here below. They are *faith, love* and *hope* (1 Corinthians 13:13). These will never be wiped out, because they are 'God qualities' and God is eternal (1 Timothy 1:17).

We were made with a deep, abiding hunger for hope. Emil Brunner said, 'As oxygen is to the lungs, so hope is to the heart.' Pierre Teilhard de Chardin wrote that, 'The world belongs to those who can offer it hope.' According to the Bible God is stubbornly hopeful about His world. Heaven itself shows that we *were* made to live happily ever after. We *were* made to live in hope of a better tomorrow.

There's one more thing to be said here. When we suffer, it would good for us to remember that, 'At the very centre of the Christian faith is the God who has suffered . . . the God spoken of in the Bible does feel our pain. He can fully sympathise because He has greatly suffered.'[11] God the Father suffered the loss of His Son; God the Son suffered the cross; God the Holy Spirit suffers each time a human being spurns His call to salvation. And yet, in it all, He remained (and remains) full of faith, hope and love!

REFERENCES:

1. Steve Taylor, *I Predict 1990* (Myrrh Records, 1987).
2. Josh McDowell, *Evidence that Demands a Verdict* (Here's Life Pub., 1979), p.81.
3. Ibid., pp.81–85.
4. Ibid., pp.85–86.

5. Ibid., pp.39–43.
6. Ibid., p.43.
7. Quoted by Josh McDowell, ibid., p.197.
8. Quoted by Lane T. Dennis, *The Letters of Francis Schaeffer* (Kingsway, 1986), p.106.
9. Bruce Springsteen, *Tunnel of Love* (CBS, 1987).
10. Quoted by Lane T. Dennis, op. cit., p.106.
11. John Dickson, *A Sneaking Suspicion* (St Matthias Press, 1992), p.26.

STUDY GUIDE

---

*Sociologists have found that 98% of all people ask the 'why?'
question from time to time in their lives—the other 2% are
unconscious.*

Professor Claudius Fritzenbacher III
Emeritus Professor,
Dept. of Verifiable Myths, Camford University.

Warm-ups
What issues concern you most when you read the
newspapers/magazines or watch TV? What is it about
these issues, specifically, which makes you angry?

Study/Discussion
Read Lamentations 3:31–33 and Hosea 6:1–7. What do
these passages of the Bible tell us about the nature and
character of God?

Read Job 31:35–37 and 38:1–7; 40:8; 41:11. What do
you think God is trying to teach Job here? What lesson can
we learn from this?

Read Ephesians 2:1–7 and John 3:18a. Does God
bring suffering into the lives of His people to punish them?

Further research project: make a brief study of the historical references to Jesus which come from sources outside
of the Bible. (See 'Other Resources' below.)

Getting Started
Take a look at your own situation. What injustices are you

suffering right now? Knowing that you are largely a product of your decisions, what can you do to improve your situation?

Further Resources

Josh McDowell, *Evidence that Demands a Verdict* (Here's Life Publishers, 1979), pp.81–87.
Paul Little, *Know Why You Believe* (Anzea Books, 1971), pp.80–89.

3

DID MOTHER TERESA SEE A CAREERS COUNSELLOR?

– WHAT SHOULD I DO WITH MY LIFE? –

There's one major difference between you and a cornflakes packet! No matter what it does (assuming a cornflakes packet can 'do' anything), it will always be the product of what others have made it. It can sit and think, 'I will be a chair, I will be a chair . . . I think I can, I think I can,' until its cardboard rots— it will remain what Mr Kellogg made it, a box for cornflakes.

YOU, ON THE OTHER hand, have the capacity to change some fairly important things about your present and your future. Sure, you can't choose your relatives, your age, or certain things about your physical appearance, but you have been gifted with the ability to make other significant choices which change your destiny. You are not simply the product of what someone else has made you.

One of the most powerful of all the choices you will make is your choice of career.

The times they are a-changing . . .

The newspaper headline read, '90 Jobs—3000 in Queue!' MacDonald's was opening a new store and needed staff. The staff manager had placed just one advertisement in a small local newspaper and when he arrived to conduct the interviews he was confronted by a line of hopefuls stretching more than a block.

Unemployment is one of the social ills of our time. Of course, there will always be a small minority of people who are not working because they have contracted 'work-aphobia', the fear of work! For these people the welfare state, despite its undoubted advantages, is a great help in their pursuit to live off the wealth of others. There are a great many more people, however, who genuinely, even desperately, want to join the workforce but can't for various reasons.

Economic recession the world over has added to the unemployment numbers in the short term. A much more telling factor is the long-term change which is taking place in the *nature* of the work available to people. The rapid spread of new technologies has meant that manual work is becoming less and less predominant—'brain' work is taking over where 'brawn' work once ruled. For those who understand and can afford the new-fangled, high-tech work tools, there are great opportunities to work from home and to specialise. Others are not so well-equipped to face the new world.

In some parts of the world these changes are wreaking havoc. In the Third World, for instance, for every job created in the cities ten people leave the rural areas. One particular capital attracts some 50,000 new inhabitants per week. These poorer countries can't provide enough housing, food and social services for their people.[1]

There are also changes in the way people see work. Even in an age where jobless numbers are high, people in the developed world are becoming more selective about the work they do. Time is becoming more important to us than money. George Barna, a marketing and research expert says that 'By the year 2000 we will have shifted to using time as our dominant indicator of value . . . we will come to believe that success is not about acquisition. It is about control [of our time].'[2]

We are looking more and more for jobs which fulfil us and help to activate our personal potential, as well as allowing us leisure time in which we can 'do our own thing.' People will tend to change jobs more in the coming years as loyalty to 'the company' is replaced by loyalty to 'me' and 'my interests'.

It's small comfort to people out of work, I know, but it seems that unemployment is always high whenever such mega-changes are taking place throughout society. The Industrial Revolution provided another example of this.

Unemployment, say the psychologists, takes people through three stages in a kind of grieving process. The first stage is shock. There are feelings of humiliation and disbelief—'how could this happen to me?' This is often followed by depression and pessimism—'this will never change!' Finally there's fatalism or stagnation—'my life's going nowhere.' To make matters worse, a new phrase 'terminally unemployed' has been invented to describe people who've little chance of long-term employment!

So what is it about work that the lack of it can be so painful?

Work—why bother?

Work offers some wonderful opportunities for a rich life (and I don't mean rich in the dollar sense). There are basically two extreme views on the place we should give to work in our lives:

1. Work's a drag and I'd rather not bother, thanks.

According to this view work is a 'necessary evil', something that wouldn't exist in an ideal world. If I could win the National Lottery or the Pools, I'd 'throw the job in' tomorrow and do something more worthwhile.

What this fails to see is the very real benefits we derive from work, such as a sense of productivity. The dictionary is the only place where success comes before work! One family therapist put it well, 'If you're unemployed and all you do is walk down to the front gate and get the paper, go to the unemployment office to look for a job, play guitar and watch TV at the end of the day, you feel unfulfilled and miserable, not worth much as a human being.'[3]

Then there's the sense of control work gives us: control over our own destiny. For a Christian that does not mean you don't exercise faith in God. What it means is that I do all *I* can and leave *the rest* to Him. Money can't buy you love, but it can bring with it a certain amount of freedom to make decisions.

Work also brings the benefits of being part of a team. There's a comradeship in the workplace—well, there should be when things are going well—which is important to our well-being. We are social beings. Work is a place to network (that's a new-fashioned word for 'making friends'!)

It's also about developing our gifts and serving the needs of the wider community in the process—which is a great feeling. I'll say more on this in a moment.

Basically, work has value because we were made to work. Not *just* to work, mind you, but there is something in us that craves meaningful employment—as opposed to meaningless drudgery. God's first gift to Adam, even before the stunning Eve appeared, was work. Adam, says John Stott, 'enjoyed perfect job satisfaction'.[4] The desire and ability to work was one of the God-like attributes Adam inherited from His Maker. God is Himself a worker. Read the first chapter of Genesis and you'll be staggered how much God achieved in a week!

It wasn't the Creation that made work hard—it was the Fall. Adam thought he could find meaning without God and that was where his work started to get him down. But now, through Jesus, God is wanting to redeem (buy back) our work, to give it the kind of joy and purpose it should have. God made work to be more than something we do to live—it should be something we *live to do!*

2. Work is the ultimate buzz and I'd like to die at the desk, thanks!

Here's the other extreme. Workaholism is a physiological and emotional addiction to the excitement, the 'high' produced by one's work. If I'm an alcoholic, I can't survive the day without frequent doses of the liquid stuff. If I'm a workaholic, or 'careerist', I can't get by for a day without making calls, sending faxes or making memos. This kind of view makes a slave to work.

Communism is probably the most work-orientated political system ever devised. Why did it fail? Oh sure, there was the Stalin syndrome—people were oppressed and as history showed they wouldn't take that for ever. But there's more to it than that. I believe communism ultimately failed because it couldn't provide the three fundamental needs at the core of human existence—the need for faith, hope and love. That's why, when the great communist walls started to crumble, people began flocking to churches and synagogues again.

Yes, one can't help feeling sorry for the communists! But wait, just before we pat our capitalist selves on the back, there's one thing our system often shares with that of communism. Both can make people the servants of a materialistic view of life. Life consists of what I possess. My status and worth come out of how well I produce.

In a book called *Your Work Matters to God,* Sherman and Hendricks tell us that boredom and busyness are two parts of the same thing—a lack of meaning and purpose. 'Work,' they say, "has become the new religion of our generation." '[5] Because we've lost the ability to relate work back to God, we try to derive meaning from the work itself. In the process we often become overworked and burn out.[6] Or we chop and change from job to job, looking for the ultimate buzz.

Alternatively, we try to 'wine and dine', or 'leisure and pleasure' our way to a sense of purpose. Our working hours are spent with one end in mind, providing the 'bucks' for a weekend of partying.

Yes, time off is important. For too many people, work takes up only 50 per cent of their time but 95 per cent of their energy! That's why God invented the day off. He gave us the Sabbath, that one day which should be set aside for rest ('hand me another Coke . . . '), reflection

('what have I really accomplished this week?') and relationships ('yes, I know you're my wife, but what was your
name again?').

Some of us though start to idolise our leisure time. We
live to find meaning in the exciting experiences we can
string together. Sadly, leisure can then become a real drag,
because we are what Sherman and Hendricks call 'hollow
men', for whom 'leisure is a liability'—it just gives us more
time to think about how pointless everything seems![7]

Work and the material products leisure can bring will
never fill our deeper thirst for spiritual meaning and sig-
nificance. Work is a great servant but a rotten master.

Meaning, said a wise person, comes from knowing
who you are and whose you are. When we can get things
in perspective and relate our work and our leisure back to
God we can rest in the knowledge that the results are His
responsibility, we can leave the outcome to Him. Here's a
great line from Jaques Ellul, a French thinker: 'In reality,
man does his work and God gives to this work its meaning,
its value, its effectiveness, its weight, its truth, its justice—
its life—and if God does not give this . . . nothing remains
of the work of man.'[8]

OK, so how did Mother Teresa know what to do with her life?

How do we figure out what we should make our life's
work—or at least our work for the next few years? As
things go these days, this may well be a choice you'll make
not once but a number of times during your life. 'By the
year 2000,' says George Barna, 'the average adult will
make four to six career changes.'[9]

Again, one of the best things about being a Christian is that I can ask for divine help with the main questions about life. If you've been around the Christian scene for a while, you will have heard people talking about God 'using' them in different ways. It's sounds a bit mercenary, I know, but it basically means that God has a design for each one of us and a plan for how we can best use the gifts He's given us. Francis Schaeffer saw it like this, 'The beautiful thing is that [God] uses us, but never in the way a soldier would use a gun only to throw it down and take another. He uses us, but He always *fulfils* us at the same time.'[10]

The key to making a good career choice, whether it's your first or your fourth, is to see that it *is* your decision, but it's one you don't have to make without help. It's not all up to God—*you* must do some thinking for yourself and about yourself if you're going to find the right career path. But there are clear biblical principles to assist you in making the right choices.

Life is a football field!

Picture this—your life is a football field. I'm writing this towards the end of a World Cup year, so I'd better make it a soccer pitch. The field is square. It has four boundaries, which we'll look at shortly. The name of the field is 'The Glory of God'.

'You can't play this game of career choice without first getting yourself onto the right field. You need to decide that your life is going to be lived for the honour of God's name and the building of His kingdom here on this little planet—the extension of His good and just rule among men. That's where Karl Marx and others have gone off the track. They've been playing on the wrong field. They've forgotten that we should first aim to please and delight God with our work, not just to find personal freedom or build some great state. Pleasing Him is a sure way to please yourself in the end (Psalm 37:4)!

Once you've made that first crucial decision, you can check out the layout of the ground. It looks like this:

NEEDS

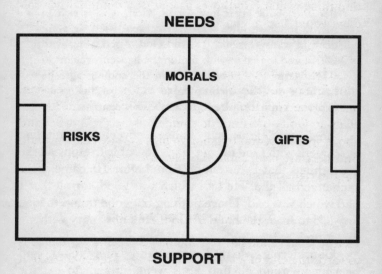

MORALS

RISKS

GIFTS

SUPPORT

The centreline: is it moral?

This is the first question I should ask of any prospective career: does it compromise morality? For Christian people, Ephesians 2:12–13 holds a great truth. It tells us that we were once 'separate from Christ, excluded from citizenship in Israel and foreigners to the covenants of the promise, without hope and without God in the world. But now in Christ Jesus you who once were far away have been brought near through the blood of Christ.'

Ephesians 2:3–7 says that we were once 'gratifying the cravings of our sinful nature and following its desires and thoughts'. Because of that we were 'objects of [God's] wrath'.

But it goes on:

> Because of his great love for us, God, who is rich in mercy, made us alive with Christ even when we were dead in transgressions . . . And God raised us up with Christ and seated us with him in the heavenly realms in Christ Jesus . . . in order that in the coming ages he might show the incomparable riches of his grace expressed in his kindness to us in Christ Jesus.

Good News! Jesus has made a covenant, a binding agreement with God for me. I am now able to enjoy all the good things that I was cut off from before He came. Jesus exchanged all that He had which was good, for all that I had which was bad. I have nothing but good things to look forward to from the hand of God. He's not angry with me any more!

Considering where I now stand before God, and bearing in mind all that Jesus went through to get me there, why would I want to throw all that away by spending my time and gifts (both of which God gave me) in pursuit of things which put me back where I came from—in the dirt?

If I want God to smile on my work, I should never accept a position which calls on me to exploit other people. For example, I wouldn't work in the prostitution or pornography 'industries'—*or* make any use of these 'services'(!)—because they exploit people sexually. I wouldn't stay in a job which I know is exploiting people economically, by causing poverty or paying inadequate wages. I'm not going to be too keen on any career which exploits people psychologically or emotionally either, as is the case in certain sections of the media industry.

Of course, within any industry there are areas a Christian will be concerned about. They provide us with opportunities to change things for the better, to live prophetically—calling something of God's vision of the future into place *today.* But if, after we've done what we can, things still don't change and we are being asked to do things which compromise our integrity, we should say the magic words, *'bye-bye!'*

Boundary one: Does it meet needs?

A young woman said to Mother Teresa, 'You couldn't pay me to do what you do!' To which the 'old saint' replied with a sly grin, 'Me neither!'

Great answer! You see, we each need something to live *on,* but we also need something to live *for!* Nothing, but nothing, can replace the joy of doing something which helps others. The Man of Nazareth knew something when He said it's better to give than to receive.

I had the promotions director of Freedom From Hunger, a secular relief organisation, sitting in my office. He told me that, while he was not a practising Christian himself, he appreciated what I believed. During his travels to some of the poorer countries of the world he had seen many Christians going about their charity work with no thought of thanks or recognition.

'If it wasn't any religious conviction, what was it that led you to this kind of work?' I asked.

'Well, I started my working life as a geologist,' he replied. 'I was making a lot of money for a while. I actually got near the top of the tree in my profession.'

'So what happened?'

'I had been involved with Freedom From Hunger as a volunteer worker for some years,' he explained. 'One day they asked me to go on a field trip overseas, to see first-hand the work they were doing in poorer countries. So I did—and it changed my life.

'I knew I couldn't go on as before. I gave up the old job and came to work for this group full-time. I've never been happier!'

This man wasn't a Christian, but he felt the heart of Christ. Bob Pearce, founder of World Vision, was asked how you become a great person. His reply? 'Find out what breaks the heart of God and pray that it breaks yours also.' Greatness begins with passion. Great movements are started out of great emotion. Great people are stirred by great feelings.

I asked the famous German evangelist Reinhard Bonnke what motivates him. He answered, 'Mal, I just see what the devil is doing to people and I get so angry!'

Ask yourself—does the career I'm considering meet any real needs? Does it contribute to a better society in which people can live more freely? Does it allow me to live for something which carries on even when I die? Ask the same questions about some of the things you do in your 'spare time'. As working hours shrink and more people fill part-time positions, we're going to need to find new ways to make our spare time useful.

'But I'm just a carpenter,' you say. 'What can God do with a carpenter?' Read the Gospels!!

Boundary two:
Does it develop my gifts?

In many books on career choices, this one would have been listed first. It shouldn't be first, but it *is* important.

I was praying in a motel room in New Zealand a while back. I was to speak at a major conference and wanted to tap into the power supply again and recharge the batteries. I got more than I bargained for—I had one of those 'Close Encounters of the Most Uncomfortable Kind'. I was asking the Boss why things weren't going as well as I had planned. I mean, I was a Christian leader, a fairly well-known speaker, and people just didn't seem to see my potential. There was a dream in me no one else seemed to share.

Well, I should have shut up, because 'Dad' gave me one of those gentle rebukes He's so good at.

'Son,' I felt He was saying, 'you have a gift in you. I have entrusted it to you. It's important to Me. But *you* are accountable for that gift, no one else. *You* must believe in its potential; *you* must do what needs to be done to give it maximum exposure. That's what *you* will answer for!'

I picked my jaw up off the floor and thought long and hard about the implications of this one. I couldn't get away with excusing failure by blaming others. I had to become more serious about my gifts. That's God's desire for all of us—that we live accountable lives.

Dr James Dobson a leading American writer and speaker, has said that he draws great motivation from the knowledge that this day might well be his last. He tries to live each day to the maximum. Does the work you are doing allow you to make use of your God-given talents? Does it help you hone those special skills? What will you have to present your Maker with when He looks for a return on His investment in little ol' you?

And we're not just talking about 'spiritual gifts'. Did you ever see *Chariots of Fire*? Great film, wasn't it? Do you remember the scene where Eric Liddell's sister is giving him a 'good dressing down' for training to run in the Olympics?

'You're not giving enough time to your real call, the mission we're running,' she complains. 'God made you to be a missionary, Eric.'

His answer is, as we Aussies sometimes say, a 'bottler'. 'Aye, Jenny,' he says, 'God made me to preach. But He also made me to run *fast*, and when I run I feel His pleasure!'

Here's a guy who really understood his giftedness. God is the source of all natural talent. *Any* ability I have is only on loan to me. Even a hobby—which is really what running was to Eric—can be something which develops a God-given potential to the maximum, and provides some good therapy too. Do you cultivate healthy interests outside the office or classroom?

One of the great things any job should do is to help develop skills in building relationships. For some people, machines have become their 'best friends'. They spend every day of their working lives 'interfacing' and 'dialoguing' with microchips.

God made you for more than that. Don't allow any job

to put you where you can't build team relationships and social friendships. And don't let your leisure time be too wrapped up with staring at a TV screen or 'talking' to a terminal!

You may also have leadership gifts. These are becoming more and more important in the workplace, as people are looking for leadership more than management. Management gets the job done by controlling things, leadership brings out the best in people by allowing them to take risks and learn hands-on. Leadership is a gift; if it's one of your talents, aim for a job which allows you to develop it.

Boundary three: Does it support me?

OK, so this one sounds too basic? You want your money back, right? Well, hang on. Think about it. God hates poverty. It demeans human beings who are made in His image—His special creation—it pulls their dignity down into the mud. It reflects more the nature of Satan, the robber, than God the restorer. He wants me to *have* because He loves me. It's His nature to give. He is even generous with those who don't acknowledge Him (Matthew 5:45)!

He also wants me to learn the joy of giving—He wants to share a good thing. But how can I obey His call to give if I have nothing in the kitty, or under the mattress? Zero divided by zero will always be zero. God wants me to have so that I can give. Much of His giving, though, will come not through the 'miracle envelope in the letterbox'. You know the scenario—you need £8 million by yesterday so that you can go save the whole of Rwanda overnight! You go to the letterbox thinking, 'This is my last chance. If God doesn't come through today, all is lost.' You open the box and find . . . yes . . . it's a *miracle!* £8 million in cold hard cash!

Now that kind of thing does happen, occasionally—God's into surprises—but it's the exception not the rule. Most of His provision comes through His blessing the work of my own hands (Deuteronomy 28:12). If there's one thing God hates more than poverty which is caused by human exploitation, it's poverty caused by laziness (2 Thessalonians 3:10–12)! If I am able to work for my food, I should. Even when God dropped bread from heaven, He required that the people go out and do the gathering (Exodus 16).

So if the work you're doing doesn't meet your own needs, you may need to pray and look for a better position.

Boundary four:
Does it allow me to take faith risks?

There's no avoiding it, ladies and gentlemen. It's there in black and white, 'And without faith it is impossible to please God.' (Hebrews 11:6) Not *improbable,* not *slightly possible* or *almost impossible,* but *impossible*! So this 'faith' thing is pretty important. What is faith?

Faith is daring to go where no human being has ever gone before! Faith is letting go of the shore so that you can discover new oceans. Faith is unleashed creativity. Does your job allow you to be a little creative now and then—or are you *content* to screw the same caps onto bottles day-in-day-out? Are you able to find new solutions to old problems—or do you always have to work by the book?

George Bernard Shaw said, 'Reasonable men adjust to their world. Unreasonable men refuse to adjust to their world. Therefore progress can only be made by unreasonable men.' Does your work allow—no, encourage—you to be unreasonable every now and then, to push the envelope on the way things are 'normally' done? (The last words of a dying employee, 'It's never been done this way before!')

Here's the bottom line folks—*faith is taking a risk to do what God tells you to do.* Many Christians complain that God never speaks to them. The problem is that they often haven't recognised His voice when He has spoken. Believe it, *whenever God tells you do to something, you'll be required to take a risk.* Any new job should allow the chance to take faith risks. It might be the risk I take in sharing my faith with a co-worker, or praying for a sick colleague, or giving to a comrade in need. It might be the risk of going on a missions trip with my church or a group like YWAM. It could be the risk of gaining extra training in discipleship. It might be the risk of heading up a small group or a department within my church.

It might be the risk of giving dangerously—sowing finances into some person's need or some ministry, beyond the call of duty. It could be any number of things the Lord will want me to do. My work environment should allow for those risks.

I know, you'll never find a job that lets you have everything you want—but where's the harm in trying to get as close as possible? Here's a great summary of what we should be looking for: 'Work is the expenditure of energy (manual, mental or both) in the service of others, which brings fulfilment to the worker, benefit to the community and glory to God.'[11]

Even a menial job can be turned to good advantage if you see it through the zoom-lens of faith. On a walk through the countryside, a man passed by a stone quarry. Three men were digging there and sweat was pouring down their backs. Being a curious cat by nature, the man stopped and asked the first worker: 'What are you doing?'

'I'm breaking rocks,' he replied gruffly.

Approaching the second worker he asked the same question. 'I'm making £200 per week,' was the answer this time.

When he came to the third labourer he expected a similar answer. But he was in for a pleasant surprise. This brawny guy stuck his chin into the air, thrust his chest forward and said: 'Can't you see? I'm helping to build a cathedral!'

How far ahead can you see with *your* job?

REFERENCES

1. Anthony Campolo, *Partly Right* (Word Books, 1985), p.171.
2. George Barna, *The Frog in the Kettle* (Regal Books, 1990), pp.39–40.
3. Mal Fletcher, *Youth: The Endangered Species* (Word Books, 1993), p.90.
4. John Stott, *Issues Facing Christians Today* (Marshall Pickering, 1984), p.166.
5. Sherman and Hendricks, *Your Work Matters to God* (NavPress, 1987), p.199.
6. Ibid., p.201.

7. Ibid., p.202.
8. Jacques Ellul, *The Presence of the Kingdom* (Helmers and Howard 1989), p.97.
9. George Barna, op cit., p.104.
10. Lane T. Dennis, *The Letters of Francis Schaeffer* (Kingsway, 1985), p.124.
11. John Stott, op. cit. p.173.

STUDY GUIDE

Independent studies have shown that chronic workaphobia is best cured by getting a good job. There is no known cure for workaholism (but we're working hard on it!).

Professor Claudius Fritzenbacher III
Emeritus Professor,
Dept. of Verifiable Myths, Camford University.

Warm-ups

If you could freely choose any job in the world, without restriction, what job would it be? What is it about that career which excites or interests you?

Study/Discussion

George Barna says, 'By the year 2000 we will have shifted to using time as our dominant indicator of value . . . we will come to believe that success is not about acquisition. It is about control [of our time].' What are the implications of this for our leisure activities? List some principles which you think we should work to when it comes to choosing how we spend our leisure time.

Read Deuteronomy 28:1–12; 2 Thessalonians 3:10–12 and Exodus 16. What do you think each of these passages tell us about God's attitude to our work?

Imagine an unemployed friend comes to see you feeling depressed about being out of work for a long period. What practical advice can you give your friend on how to keep a positive outlook?

Getting Started

Take another look at the 'football pitch' in this chapter. On a scale of 1 to 5 (very poor to very good), how does your present job or career plan match up with each of the areas listed?

Write up a list of goals and strategies which might help you get from where you are now to the kind of job you'd really like to have. (Goals are 'what' you want to do, but strategies are 'plans to get there'.)

Further Resources

Sherman and Hendricks, *Your Work Matters to God* (NavPress, 1987).

Film: *Chariots of Fire*. (What differences are there in the motivations behind the two key runners?)

Mal Fletcher, *Get Real* (Word Books, 1993), chapter 1 (on vision).

Loren Cunningham, *Daring to Live on the Edge* (YWAM Publishing, 1991).

4

WHAT'S LOVE
GOT TO DO WITH IT?

– A GUIDE TO HOLISTIC SEXUALITY –

*'Put the sizzle back in your sex life! . . . There's
nothing more thrilling than passionate lovemaking! . . .
Now you can rejuvenate your love life and reach new
heights of sexual pleasure with 'Loving Better', a three-
volume video series for adults only . . . a psychiatrist,
author and sex therapist . . . guide you throughout the
series, explaining the 'sexually explicit' lovemaking techniques demonstrated for you by a variety of couples . . .
All videos are shipped to you in a discreet,
confidential package.'*[1]

THIS WAS THE TEXT for a full-page magazine
advertisement for sex videos. The picture with it
featured a young couple locked in a steamy
embrace, apparently about to do 'what comes naturally'.
What was the magazine? Was it an adults-only, still-
wrapped-in-cellophane glossy? No, it was the weekend
magazine from one of Australia's finest family newspapers.
It was the product of a place which called itself a 'research'
institute.

The selling of sex used to be an industry for back alley

operators with slicked-down hair and sleazy minds but now the marketing of sex has gone mainstream, it's big business. We've university-educated 'sexperts' who have their own talk-shows on TV and radio, with names like 'Dr Feelgood' and 'Pillowtalk'. They promise to help us sort out our problems with sex, but what they're mostly doing is fuelling our obsession with sex and feeding on our insecurities. Advertisements in newspapers feature beautifully proportioned super-hunks and super-babes from some mythical, pimple-free planet. Their enticing smiles and provocative poses invite us to experience the sexual pleasure the product can bring—and the product might be something as unsexy as garden mulch!

Even prostitutes have a new-found respectability. Some even prefer to be called 'sex workers' or 'therapists'. On the front page of a leading newspaper there was an article announcing that people could soon buy shares in the city's leading brothel.

So how is all this 'sexationalism' helping us in our quest for a better life? Are we building healthier, stronger relationships as a result of this constant exposure to erotic things? People today have more gadgets than ever to help them communicate, and more courses to teach them how to relate to each other, yet there's probably never been a time in history when people communicate less! Loneliness has reached epidemic proportions in the Western world.

In Sydney a woman's badly decomposed body was found in the front room of her small inner suburban house. She was in her mid-sixties when she died, but the body was not discovered until three years later! This woman had lived in the area for decades, but nobody missed her for three years! *That's loneliness.*

A mother rang me on a major radio programme one evening to tell me her two teenage girls had walked out on her that afternoon. Her voice was filled with despair as she shared her years as a single mum trying to do the best she could for her children. She just didn't understand them any more, she said, and they didn't understand her. 'I'm so angry and depressed,' she cried, 'I could walk out on to the motorway and end it all tonight.' She had nobody to talk to in her hour of greatest need except a radio announcer and me, two perfect strangers she could only 'meet' on the phone. *That's loneliness.*

In America today, the average family consists of a married couple with one child. At least one of the parents is likely to have been divorced, or will be divorced. And the trend now is for 'blended families', where children are brought together from previous marriages. Sixty per cent of the children born in 1990 will live in single-parent households for some part of their lives before they reach eighteen years of age.[2] Why *are* we so poor at building relationships which last?

All the lonely people . . .

There are four major cancers afflicting modern relationships, especially those of the sexual variety:

1. Selfishness
Listen to the songs on the radio about love (or, as it is in rock 'n roll, 'lerv'). What do you hear? 'I want your sex', 'you turn me on', 'I couldn't live without you'. There's one common denominator, 'me'! We're a generation of consumers—we use and discard things. Hugh MacKay, a

leading Australian sociologist, has called this generation of young people an 'indulged generation'. He says many people today treat relationships the same way they treat things—when one breaks down or doesn't please them any more they go shopping for another. Some other sociologists are telling us that the Yuppie (Young Urban Professional) of the eighties has now given way to the 'Iddie' (I Deserve It) of the nineties. Many of us think the world owes us something, that we ought to have at least as much as our parents, and probably more. In the process, relationships have become more about what we can receive than what we can give.

According to many futurologists things might not improve in a hurry. These researchers are predicting, for example, that remarriage will occur more often in future as people continue to move out of one relationship and into another. This will happen especially at transitional stages in life, such as when the children start leaving home, or when retirement comes around. Wives will discover they have nothing in common with their husbands, men will fall 'out of love' with the wives of their youth. So they'll up and move.

That's not to say, of course, that when people tie the knot in future they don't *want* their marriages to work. Nobody really goes to the altar thinking: 'Hey, it won't last but, well, it's a nice way to spend an afternoon.' It's just that if you're a committed individualist ('me first please') you're also prone to be a short-term thinker ('who cares about tomorrow, seize the day!'). The same futurologists are also warning that real friendships will seem harder to come by and loneliness will increase. Is that so surprising?

2. Control

With the drive for individualism, say future-researchers, will come a hunger for control. People will increasingly measure their success not by how many material things they own, but by how much control they have over their circumstances. In choosing a job, for example, we'll become less concerned about income and more concerned about freedom. We'll want jobs which allow us time to do the things we enjoy doing, both at work and in our growing leisure time. Our lives will be built more and more around services and machines which allow us to have what we want now.

Already we are becoming control freaks: we expect to be able to change things at the push of a button. But we can't control other people the way we control machines. Relationships suffer when we try to manipulate other people's feelings to get our own way. That's when we kill our friendships by playing the martyr ('You don't really love me, you never really loved me . . . ') or dictator ('If you don't do what I say, I'll . . . ').

3. Flaky value systems

Picture this: an Olympic high-jumper is about to go for gold. He has the potential to be the best. He's had better training than anyone, more opportunities to develop his gift and less distractions. Everybody senses it—this is his day, major world records are about to be smashed. The crowd rise to their feet as he begins his first jump. He clears the bar easily, but that was just the warm-up. Now he's lining up for the real thing.

The crowd hold their breath, sensing that a whole new standard is about to be set. The jumper runs to the bar

with long, easy strides. He's about to launch forth
. . . here he goes . . . hang on . . . *what's this?* He's stopped
a few inches from the bar! *What's he doing?* He's casually
taking the bar from its pegs and lowering it—yes, *lowering
it*—by six inches. Now he's going back and running in
again. Of course he clears it easily, but while he stands on
the other side congratulating himself the crowd go home
in despair. What a loser!

That's how it is with us today, morally speaking. We're
a generation loaded with potential. We're capable of great
things but we stop at the bar and lower our standards to
make things that bit easier for ourselves. We sell ourselves
short and all heaven and history sigh at the waste.

In the sixties, young people raved on about the new
age which was dawning, the Age of Aquarius, when all war
would cease and everyone would wear pretty flowers in
their hair. Some very positive things came out of that
decade, but it wasn't all flower-power and harmony. One
of the things we lost back then was a respect for the morals
of our forefathers. Young people saw the inconsistencies in
governments and leaders and decided that everything 'old'
(pre-sixties) must be wrong, or stifling to their creativity. So
the proverbial baby was tossed out with the bathwater.

Now the children of those who grew up in the sixties
have no real moral roots. Today we think of right and
wrong in terms of whatever suits most people most of the
time. There are very few absolute rights and wrongs, there
are few 'commandments'. We're making things up as we
go along. We're into 'flexible traditions' and 'user friendly'
morals. We won't put up with moral standards which don't
fit our easygoing lifestyles, so we only accept morals which
don't push us too hard. We talk about society as if things

were constantly evolving into something better, but what's really happening is that we're starting to behave more like the animals it is said we came from. We do things more and more 'on instinct', without stopping to think about the moral consequences of our actions. Instead of our value systems shaping us, we change them whenever it suits us. So change is the only constant in many of our lives—and we wonder why relationships don't last.

Alexander Solzhenitsyn has these sobering words for our generation, 'All the celebrated technological achievements of progress, including the conquest of outer space, do not redeem the twentieth century's moral poverty.'[3]

4. Escape into technology

Another challenge before us is that we're losing some of our social skills because we 'talk' so much to computers and other machines. There are a lot of people for whom 'George', their IBM-compatible desktop, is their only real 'buddy'. He'll play games with them, show them films they like and even play their favourite music. The one thing George won't do is hassle them or make demands. Even when we do actually talk to other people these days it's often through the agency of George and his fellow-machines. 'Face-to-face' has given way to 'interface'. High-tech is a great servant, but a rotten master.

Sexy lies . . .

'There's nothing more thrilling than passionate lovemaking!' So said the advertisement at the start of this chapter. What does that say for the people who can't find a sexual partner or those who—shock, horror!—have actually

chosen to remain celibate? A major new study in America has found that at least 3 per cent of the adult population has never had sex. That's a higher percentage of the population than those who claim to be homosexual (2.7 per cent for men, 1.3 per cent for women)![4]

And what about those who are forced to be celibate because of some injury, disability or disease? Are they destined to a life without the ultimate thrill; is life for them a huge anti-climax, just because they don't indulge in sexual intercourse? *Get real!* There's more to life than sex.

But that's one of our problems today? We're pre-occupied with sex. Do these song lyrics sound familiar, *'I love you so much baby, that I want to sit down and have a good long talk?'* No? That's because no such song exists—or if it does, nobody's giving it airtime! According to the songs all the most rewarding relationships are sexual in nature. You can tell you're really loved and needed if you're in the sack with someone.

We've put sex on such a high pedestal that it can't live up to our expectations! Sigmund Freud (Siggie to his mates) had a lot to do with our modern preoccupation with sex. He taught that our character and behaviour are shaped by powerful, repressed influences from our past. Of all these influences he said the sexual ones are the most potent. Freud made sex seem the most important drive in our lives.

Most of the time we expect too much from sex. We build up hopes of finding just the right guy or the right girl to do 'it' with. We go out hunting for the perfect mate, the one who will ring all our chimes and make the earth move for us. But whenever we 'try it on' with someone new, we find ourselves becoming a little more jaded and disappointed. Or a little more careless about the other person's needs. Our experience never seems to match our dreams.

That's because real intimacy does *not* happen 'overnight'! And there's more to it than physical nakedness. Just because you got inside someone's bed, doesn't mean you've made it inside their head!

'But I don't want that kind of intimacy yet,' some will say. 'I just want to have a good time before I make those commitments.' Hey, do you know what several studies have shown? That every time a person indulges in sexual intercourse outside the bounds of a life-long commitment they are reducing their chances of ever finding that deeper, soul-mate intimacy. Research around the world has shown that couples who have regular sexual intercourse before marriage are more prone to break-up after marriage. They just don't develop the same respect for each other, and they are often more selfish in their expectations of one another. They also carry into their relationship vivid memories of sex with other partners. Relationships can be tricky enough, without that kind of excess baggage. That's not to say that you can't make a relationship born in these circumstances work. It's just harder in most cases.

Fulfilling sexual experience has a lot to do with a high level of trust. This kind of trust is greatly enhanced by exclusivity; you're more inclined to trust when you know your partner hasn't shared their sexual favours around but has had the character strength to hold back.

Safe . . . in more ways than one

Then there's all the talk about 'safe sex'. *In some ways this is probably the sexual con-job of the century!* I say that for three reasons. Firstly, because condoms are not as safe as some trendy magazines will lead you to believe. They do tend to slip during intercourse, allowing fluids to get through. Even if the condom holds, most condom manufacturers claim that at best their product has only an 80 per cent success rate, and very often it's much lower. You're only protected from sexually transmitted diseases (STDs) eight times out of ten *at best*. Is that *really* good enough for you?

Secondly, those who preach the benefits of 'safe sex' never tell you much about your other options, like abstinence for example. I saw an advertisement promoting safe sex in a well-respected glossy magazine. It featured a full-page photo of a condom. The headline read, 'The Only Thing Between You And AIDS.' Then, in very small print and buried in the middle of a long paragraph, it said, 'Aside from saying "no", a condom is the only thing preventing you from catching AIDS.' In many sex education classes at high school, pupils are shown in graphic detail how to put on a condom, but they hear only a few words about abstinence.

Saying 'no' *is* the best form of prevention for STDs. Yet it only gets into the small print. Why? Because those who publish these ads and run many of these classes believe that no young person *wants* to—or *can*—say 'No' to sex before marriage. They say to themselves, who would *want* to remain a virgin? Actually there are many people who choose to see their virginity as a treasure rather than a mill stone. They see their sexual purity as a gift from God, not a handicap or disability. They've decided to give their virginity away only to their chosen marriage partner, as a symbol of their special, exclusive love for that person.

In the Bible the word translated as 'virgin' is from another word which means 'one who is separate and set aside'. *To be a virgin is to be set aside, not to be left out!* It's an honourable thing. Hey, even people who've lost their virginity tend to respect guys and girls who've had the strength and guts to hold on to theirs.

As for the idea that young people cannot say 'no' to sex, well that's just downright demeaning to this generation. It's an insult to their will power. It assumes that young adults today have no more stamina than some of their parents!

The third reason I say the 'safe sex' campaign is a con-job is that it fails to talk about any aspect of sex aside from the physical. That's a very important part, sure, but if you've studied third form biology you know that your sex drive springs not from your sex organs, but from hormones released by the pituitary gland which is in the brain. Sex drive begins above the shoulders, not below the hips! Sex is something which involves the whole person: brain, emotions and spirit. *Safe sex has to be safe psychologically, emotionally and spiritually too.*

Many people are being conned into thinking that promiscuity is a sign of great independence of thought—when it's actually a symbol of conformity. 'In no other civilisation has man been so totally repressed,' says philosopher Jacques Ellul. Our civilisation tries to dominate human beings, he claims. It allows them some limited options about the use of their time and so on, to make them feel like the masters of their fate, but in reality it brings pressure on them to conform in more important things.[5]

But there are still some rebels out there (and you can join them)!

In August–September 1994 an enthusiastic horde of teenage girls and boys drove short stakes into the grass in the green mall in front of the Washington Monument. Attached to each of 211,163 stakes was a card on which a young American had put his or her name to pledge. The vow read like this, 'Believing that true love waits, I make a commitment to God, myself, my family, those I date, my future mate and my future children to be sexually pure until the day I enter marriage.' *Life* magazine published pictures of the coloured cards stretching off into the distance. Young people from 150 countries around the world are enrolling for what's become known as the 'True Love Waits' campaign.[6] *Vive La Revolution!*

What does God know about sex?

So, you think the Bible is a boring, stuffy, nothing-goes book when it comes to the subject of sex? Have you ever read the book of the Bible called 'Song of Solomon' (or 'Song of Songs')? It's a full-on celebration of sex within marriage. *Are there any pictures?* No, because it doesn't need them! Without crudeness, it graphically describes the joyful experience sex is meant to be between a husband and wife.

It's important to say here that old-fashioned, don't-talk-about-it attitudes to sex are *not* based on Bible teaching. The Bible is very frank about sexual experience. It doesn't treat sex as a taboo subject, or as if it were something from the gutter. In fact, it dignifies sex by saying that it was God's great creative idea in the first place. (*Playboy* didn't invent sex!) The Bible doesn't hide anything, it just refuses to elevate sex beyond its proper place in our lives.

All of the Bible's teaching on sexual relationships is

based on what it has to say about marriage. Marriage was created to be the closest of all human friendships. In God's eyes, *dating is meant to lead to courtship*. Dating is about making a friend, but courtship is the process of getting to know someone you hope to marry. People of the opposite sex whom you date should never suffer the indignity of being looked upon as pieces of meat. They should be seen as prospective life partners. Of course even in a marriage things are not all a bed of roses. A wedding album and a marriage certificate won't guarantee that you'll never feel lonely again or that you'll always feel close to your partner. But marriage is still the best way of providing the kind of security and trust needed in a fulfilling sexual relationship.

Whenever the Bible is negative about sex outside marriage, you have to take it in the context of the very *positive* things it has to say about sex *inside* marriage. The people who say the Bible puts down sex are actually the people who don't like its emphasis on marriage.

Marriage is not a human invention. God Himself performed the first wedding—He even played matchmaker to the bride and groom. It would have been some wedding. The garden of Eden would take some beating as a venue, for a start, and you can imagine how good that first, totally healthy couple must have looked to each other! But God didn't create marriage just so that Adam and Eve could have sex. He had much more in mind. So, what are God's intentions for marriage and sex?

1. Companionship

Why is it that most people go completely round the twist if they're cut off from contact with other human beings for any great length of time? It's because human beings were not made to be lonely. God Himself is a social Being and the nature of humanity reflects that. God is a Trinity, He is Father, Son and Holy Spirit working together in total harmony and love for each other. I don't know about you, but I find it kind of comforting to know that behind everything which exists there is a great relationship. The Bible says it very simply, 'God is love' (1 John 4:8).

That makes loneliness *unnatural* in the universe. God knows that love cannot exist on its own, it must have an object. In the light of His own nature God looked at Adam and said, 'Hey, it's not good for this guy to be alone—he needs someone of his own kind to love.' Intelligent as they are, dolphins could not provide the level of love human beings need.

2. Completion

Eve was not a plaything for Adam, and Adam was no toy-boy for Eve. She completed him, she was his complement, and he was hers. What's the point of marrying someone who thinks, feels and behaves in *exactly* the way you do? What can they add to your life, what can you ever learn from them? Life gets pretty dull if you're spending all your days looking at your own reflection.

If you're going to marry, you want to have someone around who is strong where you are weak and weak where you are strong. Fred Hartley says in his book *Men And Marriage*, 'While strengths will always be an asset to a marriage, a relationship that never gets beyond strength-to-strength attraction will never mature . . . True intimacy is only achieved when spouses allow each other to begin to touch each other strength-to-weakness.'[7] That kind of intimacy is only achieved when husband and wife put themselves in a very vulnerable position, when they're willing to really open up with each other. That takes trust, and trust takes time.

3. Commitment

Early on in the Bible, God told us what marriage is all about, 'For this reason [that is, for marriage] a man will leave his father and mother and be united to his wife' (Genesis 2:24). Another version says he will 'cleave' to his wife—that means to stick like glue. The man was to leave his old family home and totally give himself to building a new life with his bride. (See, even God understood about in-laws!)

'Hang on,' you say. 'Adam didn't have a father, or a mother.' You're right. God wanted it understood that this statement was not just for the first couple but for all those other couples who would follow in history. He was setting down His pattern for *all of us*. Marriage was to be a very special and private sharing of two lives; two people were to give themselves completely to each other, to the exclusion of all other people.

4. Consummation

So where does sex itself fit in to all this? After God had married Adam and Eve, He instructed them to come together sexually (Genesis 1:28). He actually encouraged them to sleep together! Notice, though, that sex didn't come first in God's order, it came after certain other things were in place, such as commitment. Sex didn't come first, not because it wasn't important, but because it was very important. God intended sex to be *the ultimate act of union* in a marriage. Sex was God's way for man and woman to complete (consummate) the act of marriage. He knew that sex would involve a total trusting, a complete giving of one to the other. It was to be the final seal on their commitment to each other, on their promise to be faithful.

5. Celebration

News Flash: sex is fun! It feels good—it was designed to. Adam and Eve would have had a great honeymoon: moonlit evenings, long walks along sandy beaches, and nights alone expressing their love with physical passion. God didn't stop them—after all, their sexuality was His gift to them. He didn't *eliminate* their pleasure but He did *limit* it, in the sense that He told them to enjoy it only within marriage. Sadly, many people lose the joy of their sexuality by making pleasure their god. They think that limiting sex to the marriage bed somehow spoils the fun. In many areas of life, though, limitations actually become 'liberations'.

I'll illustrate it this way. I travel a lot. I'm asked to speak at events in many different places around the world. I love the work I do and I don't even mind the travelling too much (aside from the aircraft seats made for leprechauns), but I do hate being away from my family. Whenever I'm about to go away for more than a few days I know I'm going to miss my wife Davina and my children, so I naturally try harder to pack as much as possible into our time together. Some of the very best times in our family life have been just before I've gone away or just after I've come home. I appreciate my family more because of the limitations on our time together.

That's the way it should be with our sexual experience. The limitations God has placed on us in the area of sex can actually *enhance* our appreciation of it, and make it more enjoyable for us. Even sex-researchers are now making that discovery. One study showed, for example, that the women most likely to achieve orgasm each and every time they have sex are Protestant Christians![8]

God created sex to be much more than a consumer product, a one-night-stand kind of thing. It was never meant to be a self-serving 'sport'. In sports, there are always winners and losers. Sex is supposed to be a win-win situation, giving comfort, confidence and enjoyment to both partners. Sex is meant to be the completion of a commitment to four things: to being the other person's best friend; to helping the other person develop to their full potential and allowing them to do the same for you; to devoting yourself to your partner and to giving them pleasure within an *exclusive* relationship.

Contrary to what some lobby groups are claiming, most people today understand the benefits of marriage and the importance of being faithful to your partner. Recent research by the University of Chicago has found that most Americans are monogamous—75 per cent of married men and 85 per cent of married women remain faithful to their partners.[9] So don't believe everything you read about promiscuous sex and how 'everybody's doing it'.

Looking for Mr/Ms R.I.G.H.T. . . .

Here are a few qualities to look for in your search for Mr/Ms R.I.G.H.T.:

R—Respect

Martin Buber, a Jewish theologian, taught that there are two kinds of relationship in the world—the 'I—It' and the 'I—You'. In the first instance, he said, I will treat people as if they are things, entities which exist simply for my gratification. In the latter case, however, I will recognise that other people are created with the same dignity and rights which I possess and I'll treat them accordingly. *Guess which kind of relationship is likely to last the distance.*

Aussie singer Steve Grace has a song which says, 'You're somebody, not just anybody.' That's the way we all want to be treated. In your search for a partner you want someone who looks up to you and encourages you to look up to yourself. You don't measure someone's respect for you by their promises. Whether or not they respect you can be seen in their:

1. ***Willingness to abide by the high standards you've set for yourself.*** If someone is constantly trying to talk you out of a high standard you've been aiming for—sexual abstinence for example—they're saying, 'I don't think you can make it, I don't think you're worth that much.' In other words, they're treating you as an 'It'.

2. ***Willingness to listen to you, to learn to understand your needs.*** This kind of listening goes beyond just hearing spoken words, it means catching the feelings behind the words too. It involves attending to what the other person has to say—giving them undivided attention—then feeding it back in your own words so they have opportunity to correct or affirm what you've said. Sometimes it's a good idea to set aside specific times for this kind of interaction, otherwise we can talk at each other until our gums bleed without ever really communicating.

iii) ***Respect for themselves***. You can measure that by the way they present themselves. Do they have good habits of dress, exercise and eating? (Hey, they may not dress in a tux and eat caviar, but they can do the best with what they've got.) Do they constantly speak down about themselves or have trouble accepting compliments?

Also, look at their work habits. Someone who is content to just get the job done, barely, doesn't take pride in their work or themselves. Check out their emotional state too, especially under pressure. You never really know someone until you've seen them in a crisis situation. Do they have control over their emotions, or do they crack in times of stress? If you've never seen them lose their cool, chances are you don't know them well enough. You can't be strong enough for two people, so don't fool yourself. And don't get a 'messiah complex' either—don't make it your lifelong mission to 'save' them from themselves. (Nobody can be saved who doesn't first want to be!)

The key to attracting someone who will respect you is to honour yourself, to show that you think enough of your own value to set high standards for yourself. Of course you can get too choosy, living in a fairytale land of Snow Whites and Prince Charmings which makes the real world seem filled with ugly witches and green frogs. In that case you become manipulative, putting pressure on people to come around to your way of thinking. Generally, though, it's better to err a little on the side of self-respect than self-debasement. Don't let anyone steal your self-respect.

I—Intelligence
Do you want to spend the rest of your days with a brain-dead jelly-fish? No sir! As you go about meeting new

people ask yourself this question, 'What can I learn from this person?'

You don't have to marry an astrophysicist, but the person you give your life to should be intellectually stimulating to you. They should stretch you mentally. Intelligence is not measured so much by how much someone knows, but by whether they have an enquiring mind. Curiosity is a great trait to look for. Ask—has this person developed habits of study and self-improvement which will mean they'll always have something new to offer the relationship? Do they think for themselves and work through problems logically? Don't just look for areas of common interest; find areas where your interests vary too. Remember, there's one thing you're going to share plenty of—time!

G—Goodness

Most of us want to spend our lives with someone who is wise. Someone who knows what to do in any given situation. But very few stop to think about where wisdom comes from. Are some people just born wise? Do people get wiser as they get older? I've met some eighty-year-olds who are incredibly stupid and some sixteen-year-olds who are wise beyond their years.

No, the Bible says that 'the fear of the Lord is the beginning of wisdom' (Proverbs 9:10). Wisdom begins with a right heart attitude towards God—a commitment to what pleases God, a desire for moral excellence or virtue, which is what 'goodness' means.

If a young man or woman decide they want to have a right attitude to God, to live in a way which is morally pleasing to Him, they will begin to exercise wisdom because they're allowing the One who rules the universe to rule their decisions.

How do you know someone has a good heart towards God? Partly by their attitude to people. Out of a good heart towards God will come a good heart towards people, whom God loves. That's why you should develop relationships in the context of a group of friends. It's never helpful to isolate yourself too quickly spending all your time with that one 'special person'. You need to keep your entire network of friends in place, so that you are able to grow as a person at the same time your relationship is developing.

Don't waste time trying to build a lasting bond with someone who demands that you spend all of your 'friendship time' exclusively with them. What looks like devotion to you now, will become an obsessive level of control later on.

You should be looking for a partner who is generous towards others—generous with their money, time, encouragement, prayers and forgiveness. Someone who likes to get together with other people who love God, to encourage them. Someone who is not a stuffy, holier-than-thou religious 'kook', but someone who wants to follow Jesus' example in the way they live.

I can't find a better definition of what it means to be 'good' than the one Paul gives in Philippian 4:8: 'Whatever is true, whatever is noble, whatever is right, whatever is pure, whatever is lovely, whatever is admirable—if anything is excellent or praiseworthy—think about such things.'

Look for and 'think about' a partner who matches this list and you won't go far wrong.

H—Honesty

Billy Joel sang, 'Honesty, it's such a lonely word; Everyone is so untrue . . . ' Truthfulness is absolutely essential to good relationships. You need to be honest and to expect your partner to do the same. But being vulnerable is not easy, there is a risk and that can be difficult. The night before I was married we had a wedding rehearsal. I acted so cool on the outside, but on the inside I was feeling about as comfortable as a frog in biology class! And my best man was trying to make me feel better by telling me mother-in-law jokes! I knew I was taking a risk—my fiancée was taking a bigger one—but it was a calculated risk and it was worth it.

Some risks *are* worth taking.—especially if you've been hurt before—but you need to find someone you're willing to take that risk with.

Real honesty is being willing to do what's in the relationship's best interests *even when that costs you something.* There will be times in even the closest of relationships when you'll want to correct or even rebuke your partner. The Bible tells us to speak the truth 'in love' or, as another version puts it, to speak the truth 'with the accent of love'. (Ephesians 4:15, Barclays) This means to share your views without tearing down their self-worth, to separate their behaviour from their value as a person. You need to be specific about the behaviour which upsets you, to tell them how you feel about it and then to affirm them as a person of value. ('This is what you did . . . this is how I felt about it . . . I know you'll do better next time.')

You need someone who can share openly with you. Some girls go for the strong, silent type of guy, until they find out he's silent because he's sullen and can't open up.

Some guys prefer women who jump to fulfil their every whim, until they find out the girl is subservient only because she's afraid of rejection. Honesty is not always comfortable, but it is always healthy.

T—True

Deep relationships don't just happen. They take time and commitment. Marriage is not just about the coming together of two bank accounts or two bodies. In God's eyes it's a spiritual thing, the intertwining or union of two spirits. He knows that there are days when you won't love the way your partner looks, or even their personality or sense of humour. It's a deep, spiritual union which holds a marriage together.

That's why the Bible is generally negative towards divorce. Divorce is never commanded or even encouraged in the Bible. Jesus told the religious leaders of His day that Moses' law only allowed divorce because of the hardness of human hearts, and that God never really wanted divorce to happen at all (Matthew 19:3–9).

Remarriage after divorce is not encouraged either. There are two instances where it is allowed: firstly where a person's partner has committed serious sexual immorality and secondly where a Christian has been deserted by their unbelieving partner. But even in these cases it is a last resort. John Stott sums it up, '[God's] intention was and is that human sexuality will find its fulfilment in marriage and that marriage will be an exclusive, loving and lifelong union. This is His ideal.'[10]

You need to find a partner who will commit themselves to working with you to build a spiritual union which lasts. Having someone fall in love with your spiritual side, not just your body or personality, takes time, so don't be in too much of a hurry. *Don't settle for sex on its own, when you can have sex with lifelong friendship, trust and commitment!*

REFERENCES

1. *The Australian,* weekend magazine (August 13–14, 1994).
2. George Barna, *The Frog in the Kettle* (Regal Books, 1990), pp.66–67.
3. Tom Sine, *Wild Hope* (Monarch, 1991), p.69.
4. University of Chicago report, 'Sex in America', *Time* (October 1994).
5. Jacques Ellul, *The Presence of the Kingdom* (Helmers and Howard 1989), p.63.
6. *Life* magazine, (September 1994).
7. Fred Hartley, *Men and Marriage* (Bethany House Pub. 1994), pp.116–117.
8. *Time,* op. cit.
9. Ibid.
10. John Stott, *Issues Facing Christians Today* (Marshall Pickering, 1984), p.300.

STUDY GUIDE

Recent research reveals that sex need not be a health hazard.

Professor Claudius Fritzenbacher III
Emeritus Professor,
Dept. of Verifiable Myths, Camford University.

Warm-ups

What are your top three favourite songs on the hit charts (or in your private collection) at the moment? Evaluate what each of these says about relationships generally but in particular relationships with the opposite sex.

Study/Discussion

I've said that real intimacy doesn't happen 'overnight'. In your opinion, what *is* real intimacy? How do we go about building relationships which are truly intimate?

Read 1 Corinthians 7:2–9 and Matthew 19:12. What do you think it means to say that celibacy is a 'gift'? In the light of this, how should we treat someone who has decided to remain celibate (until marriage, or for life)?

Read 2 Corinthians 11:2. What does this verse tell us about virginity as God sees it?

Read Genesis 2:24. What do you think it means, in practical terms, for a man and woman to 'be united', or 'cleave' to each other in marriage?

Look again at the section headed, 'Looking for Mr/Ms R.I.G.H.T.'. How do you think a person can go about attracting a partner who really respects them?

Getting Started

Think ahead for a moment. Imagine you have been married for ten years. What are some of the qualities you'd like to see in your marriage partner after this time?

How can you begin *now* to ensure that the kind of person you want in the long term is the kind of person you develop a relationship with in the short term?

If you're already married, how can you help your partner to become more like the kind of person you want to be married to? Be a little realistic here, won't you!

Further Resources

Listen to any of the present top five music hits. (Many are an education in what *not* to do!)

5

DOES GOD
EAT LENTIL SOUP?

– VEGGIES AND COUCH POTATOES –

*Just over two years ago, anorexia had whittled
(Tracey) Gold, the actress who played Carol in the
TV sitcom* Growing Pains, *down to a 36kg wraith
who was in danger of dying. Hard work, therapy and
nutrition counselling have slowly helped put flesh
back on her bones.*[1]

TRACEY GOLD IS twenty-five years of age. She is
living proof that even when you have all the trap-
pings of outward success, things can go terribly
wrong on the inside. And when things go wrong emotionally, our bodies suffer too.

In recent years there has been a real switch in the way
most of us regard health. We talk a lot more about 'holistic' and 'alternative' medicine which emphasises the healing of mind and emotions as well as body.

People in previous ages were quite good at understanding the interconnection of human make-up. For centuries church groups set up hospitals which not only dealt
with physical symptoms of disease, but also helped people

cope with the emotional and spiritual aspects of their lives. Emotional and physical well-being were seen to be tied together.

Then along came Sir Isaac Newton and his mechanistic view of life, and modern science started to break everything down into its separate parts. Healing became a matter of treating 'parts' of people, rather than the whole person. Now we've got heart specialists, lung specialists and so on. We tend to view our bodies as collections of little machines inside one big machine.

As far as the Bible is concerned, God has always seen us in a holistic way. The greatest of all the commandments is given in Deuteronomy 6:5 and is expanded in Mark 12:30, where Jesus says, 'Love the Lord your God with all your *heart* and with all your *soul* and with all your *mind* and with all your *strength*' (italics added). The heart is the place of decision and spiritual experience; the soul is the area for feeling; the mind is for thought and 'strength' refers to the physical body. That just about sums up all that you need to be human!

God has plans to help us in every aspect of our lives. Some of the Christian healing ministries which have sprung up around the world since the 1940s have once again reminded us that God is not just interested in the spirit of a man or woman—He wants to help in the physical area too. And very recently we've seen the emergence of another phenomenon in the church—the moving of God's Spirit in laughter. God is interested in freeing the emotions too!

I like what a medical doctor once wrote, 'The sincere acceptance of the principles and teachings of Christ with respect to the life of mental peace and joy . . . and clean living, would at once wipe out more than half the difficulties, diseases and sorrows of the human race.'[2]

Don't just sit there . . . choose something!

Fitness and health are multibillion dollar industries around the world. In America alone there are over 30 million runners, 27 million people who play tennis, ride a bike, hike or swim, and 13 million weightlifters and body builders. Think how many Nikes and Reeboks are needed to service all these people, then you get some idea of the scale of the fitness industry!

There are basically five types of exercise 'on the market' these days:

1. Aerobic
Steady, non-stop activity which quickens the heart rate and makes you sweat and breathe quickly. Examples: swimming, jogging, cycling, walking (and that stuff you see on TV leotard-sessions!)

2. Anaerobic
Low intensity, 'stop-and-go' exercise which is short in duration. Examples: tennis, golf.

3. Isotonic
Rhythmic, repetitive exercise which involves motion. Tensing and relaxing muscles improves blood circulation. Examples: calisthenics, archery, weight training.

4. Isotometric

Exercise without much movement. It basically involves lifting or pushing against an object which won't move and, though it can make you stronger, it doesn't improve your heart. Example: pushing your hands against each other.

5. Pretend

Any new 'wonder technique' which promises to make you fitter or leaner without making any effort.

What are the benefits of exercise?

Exercise improves your appetite and digestion; it gives you more energy and stamina and helps you sleep better; it increases your ability to fight off sickness and it improves your disposition (which is nice for the people who have to live with you!) It also burns off calories and peels away cholesterol which can give you major problems by clogging up your arteries, causing unpleasant things like strokes and coronaries. Have I forgotten anything? Oh yes, *it helps you look better on the beach!*

You don't need to embark on an Olympic training scheme to start feeling better. Just one brisk 30- to 45-minute walk each day, three to five times a week, can boost the activity of disease-fighting cells in your system. It *is also* possible to do too much exercise. High intensity exercise of long duration can increase the output of stress hormones such as adrenalin and cortisol, which could actually inhibit your immune system.

The best forms of exercise allow you to do several important things:

a) *Move:* To burn up calories.
b) *Stretch and breathe deeply:* To relieve tension and help you relax.
c) *Bend, twist and swing:* To develop flexibility and agility in muscles and joints.
d) *Set your own pace:* To develop at your body's own speed, not someone else's.
e) *Do aerobic activity for around fifteen minutes:* To increase your heart rate.
f) *Enjoy yourself:* To give you incentive to do it again tomorrow!
g) *Like yourself:* To help improve, not pull down, your self-esteem.

To make sure you don't overdo it while you're exercising, experts say you should run certain checks on yourself: like making sure you can talk in a normal way during most of the exercise. You should also warm up and cool down properly and learn to listen to your own body and stop when it tells you it's had enough.

But wait, before you go and spend your money on that ski outfit, there's an important question to be answered, *why?* Why do we go to all this trouble? What's the point of all this huffing and puffing? I mean, we're all going to fall off our perch one day anyway! And if you happen to be a religious type, surely you're only concerned with the hereafter and stuff like that?

Actually, Christians have the *best* reason to be healthy—*because God is into fitness and health!* Think about it— there are at least three reasons to believe that statement:

1. You're Incredible!

Some of us look in the mirror and think, 'Wow! How could such a *fantastic* person live in such a *flab-tastic* body? Maybe we did evolve from monkeys, *and I'm the missing link!*' There's always something about the way we look or feel which we don't like—'I'm so small I have to reach up to pat my dog on the head'; 'My arms are so long I get gravel rash on my knuckles,' and so on.

Louis Armstrong took a long look at the world and sang (or grunted), *What a wonderful world!* Louis was right. The world we live in is incredible!

Running throughout nature are what the scientists call 'fractal forms'. Every wave that breaks upon the beach is different from the last one, yet they all share a common pattern. Each leaf on the tree outside your bedroom is unique, yet it has the same basic pattern as the next one. Within the diversity of nature there are common threads of design. Wave patterns are different from leaf patterns, but both can be summed up in mathematical formulae, and reproduced on computers! Did all this happen by cosmic accident? No sir—God's a creative genius!

And you, yes lil' ol' you, represent the pinnacle of God's creativity. When God had finished making the natural world He said it was 'good', but when He was through making human beings, He said things were *'very* good' or the 'best' they could be (Genesis 1:31). To quote the ancient Songwriter, you are 'fearfully and wonderfully made' (Psalm 139:14).

Consider this—without any conscious effort on your part, that body of yours just keeps regenerating, day in, day out. Your skin is new every month, your liver is new every six months and your brain is new every twelve months.

(Next time someone calls you stupid, just say, 'Wait till you see me this time next year!') Yet even though you are constantly changing and growing, your make-up is fairly constant due to the incredible organising function of your DNA.

Business writers like Tom Peters are now talking about the 'Wow Factor', something possessed by that new product which is so revolutionary and so far ahead of its time that it just blows everyone's mind. When God made you He injected into creation a good dose of the 'Wow Factor'!

The stamp of God's brilliance is in you and me. And He didn't go to all that trouble to have us throw the whole deal away through either sheer neglect or self-destructive abuse! When your body and emotions are in good condition, God is glorified. Physical and mental health are gifts from God and we'll give account for what we did with them. That's a great incentive to stay as healthy as you can!

2. The Bible is a good-health book

The Bible talks a lot about health. Most of God's great human allies were blessed with good health. Moses was one such person. This man lived to be 120 years old and even then 'his eyes were not weak [and his] strength was not gone' (Deuteronomy 34:7).

Joshua was another man greatly esteemed by God. As a man of forty-five, Joshua had been sent to spy out the land of Canaan for Israeli occupation. When the Israelites finally reached this promised land and began dividing it up among their tribes, Joshua was by then eighty-five years of age. But he still demanded the right to go out and fight for the land God had promised him. He said, 'I am still as strong today as the day Moses sent me out [to spy on Canaan]; I'm just as vigorous to go out to battle now as I was then.'

Elijah was another man who did great things for God in his generation. And he was fit! In 1 Kings 18, he spent a day challenging (and beating) the occult prophets in a 'call-down-fire-from-heaven' contest. Then he took some time out for a strenuous prayer meeting on the top of Mount Carmel. He then picked up his cloak, slipped off his Doc Martens, and, assisted by the supernatural power of God, outran a chariot over a distance of about ten miles! Sign the boy up for the track team, quick!

In the New Testament, church leaders like Paul make many references to the sporting arena in their letters of instruction. For example, in 1 Corinthians 9 Paul says we should be like runners who go flat-out for the prize (verse 24); like boxers who make every blow count (verse 26); and like athletes who discipline their bodies (verse 27). In Philippians 3:14 he tells us to focus on the future, like a runner going for the finish line.

But doesn't the Bible say physical exercise is of no benefit, that God's only concerned with spiritual things? No, what it actually says is, 'Physical training is of some value, but godliness has value for all things, holding promise for both the present life and the life to come' (1 Timothy 4:8). It's not that physical training is unimportant, it's just that spiritual training is of even more benefit, because it leads to eternal life.

And, of course, Jesus did a lot for people in the area of health. Most of Jesus' public ministry life was divided between teaching and healing. He gladly and freely cured people of all kinds of diseases and pains (Matthew 4:24). On many occasions everyone who came to Him with a need was healed (Luke 6:19; 7:21). Sometimes from dawn till dusk He would be preaching and laying hands on the sick. Yet even when He was tired, and lesser men would have gone home to bed, Jesus was still willing to heal (Mark 7:24).

The Bible says a great deal about emotional healing too, but more on that later . . .

3. God loves pro-active people!

Mahalia Jackson said, 'God don't sponsor no flops!' What does that mean—that God is only glorified by people who have the perfect physique, or people without any disabilities? No. It's those who are looking for the 'perfect' physique who can get themselves into serious trouble, as we'll see in a moment. The point is that each of us, whatever condition we're in right now, should be working to improve where we can—because a desire to improve shows an *attitude* which glorifies God.

Tom Peters says, 'Powerlessness is a state of mind. If you think you're powerless, you are.'[3] Have you ever seen pictures of rats and mice that scientists use for studies into behaviour; or did you ever read about Dr Pavlov and his performing dogs?

Science has learned a lot about how human beings react by watching critters like these. But the similarity only goes so far. There's a major difference between rats, dogs and people—people are gifted with the ability to think rationally and make moral decisions based on a system of values. Animals act mainly on instinct—a certain cause will usually bring about a particular effect. They can be taught to behave in different ways through repetition, but they can't choose as humans do.

Many of us have come to believe that we are actually *like* these animals. We have a deterministic view of life—'I am a victim of what the fates dish out to me.' So we spend our lives as *reactive* people, always responding to the emergencies around us. We have a victim mentality. That's what's insulting to God—the defeatist, loser mentality which keeps many of us from exercise and healthy habits. God made us to be 'subduers', to rule over the circumstances around us (Genesis 1:28). He made us to be *proactive* people, taking the initiative to change and improve our lives wherever we can.

Vegetables and couch potatoes . . .

Up till modern times it was generally assumed that three good meals a day would be enough to give you all the vitamins you need. People didn't go to gyms or consult personal eating plans, mainly because they 'worked out' on the land and ate more home-grown, less chemically treated products. Their soil was also free of the effects of degradation caused by chemical fertilisers and overloading with metals.

Research in recent years has shown that we eat too many calories, too much salt and too much protein; and that we need more calcium, trace minerals and vitamins, especially vitamins C, A and B-complex.

In the light of this, dietitians are suggesting that we eat more fibre (fruit, vegetables and nuts), fish and poultry and less fats and oils. They also recommend that we steer clear of too much junk and processed foods, because they contain large amounts of processed carbohydrates like white sugar and white flour. And that we get ourselves some vitamin supplements.

Vitamin deficiencies have a number of causes. Some of the most common are: poor digestion (sometimes caused by eating too fast!); excessive alcohol use (inhibits the liver and pancreas which are vital to digestion); smoking; fast food; fad diets (which often miss whole food groups); stress; teenage growth spurts (especially in girls) and even lack of sunlight (working in an office all day). If you have a serious concern about your vitamin intake, you should see your doctor before you rush out and buy bottles of pills. Taking vitamins your body doesn't need gets you nowhere.

We all learned in school that a well-rounded eating plan would contain foods from each of the six major food groups. A good daily diet would look something like this:

1. Fats, oils, sweets: Taken only occasionally
2. Milk group (including cheese, cream, yoghurt): 2 servings per day
3. Meat and meat alternatives group (including chicken, fish, nuts, seeds, eggs): 1-2 servings per day
4. Fruit group: 2-4 servings per day
5. Vegetable group: 3-5 servings per day
6. Breads and cereals: 6 or more servings per day

Did you know that these six major food groups were listed in the Bible—centuries before good health became big business? Nearly 5,000 years ago God promised Israel that if they did as He asked them to He would send His blessing on them. In Deuteronomy 7:13 and 28:2–13, God promises to increase their: oil (they used olive oil instead of margarine), cattle (their milk and meat), crops (their vegetables and fruit), and their 'kneading trough' (their bread).

What does God know about nutrition?

The Bible has a great deal to say about food. One of the very first commands God gave to Adam and Eve related to eating. He told them they could eat of 'every seed-bearing plant on the face of the whole earth and every tree that has fruit' (Genesis 1:29).

Does that mean God expects us all to be vegetarians? No, because He later tells them that they can eat 'everything that lives and moves'—but they can't eat meat which has its 'lifeblood still in it' (Genesis 9:3–4). Actually, the Bible neither encourages nor forbids vegetarianism. Paul tells us that whether we eat meat or not is purely a matter of private conscience and we should not condemn each other because of what we eat (Colossians 2:16–17).

Jesus worked some of His greatest miracles with food. For example, He fed 5,000 people and later 4,000 people with no more than a few 'fish sandwiches' (Matthew 14:15–21; Matthew 15:32–39). His first miracle involved turning everyday water into instant, well-matured wine (John 2:1–11)! (If it wasn't real wine, as some people argue, why does the Master of Ceremonies say it's the best wine of the day? Was He a connoisseur of grapejuice?)

But does the Bible give any dietary advice? Well, God did tell the Israelites about what kinds of animals they were allowed to eat (Leviticus 11) and He did lay out certain dietary restrictions for people He had special plans for, like Samson (Judges 13). Sometimes it's hard to tell how many of these instructions were given for ceremonial rather than physical reasons.

But we do know that some of God's most honoured servants deliberately disciplined their bodies, choosing carefully the kinds of food they ate, and came out looking much fitter for it. Take Daniel, for example. This young prince-in-exile and his three closest friends placed themselves on a strict vegetables-and-water diet for ten days. Then they showed themselves to their captors looking, 'healthier and better nourished than any of the young men who ate the royal food' (Daniel 1:15). As a result these fitness-conscious guys were allowed to stay on their special regimen for the whole of their three-year 'reorientation period' in Babylon. They became the standard for every one else to match. (*Note:* They did not go on any 'fad' diet, they simply disciplined themselves in what they ate.)

Generally speaking, there are no specific eating plans in the Bible, for two very simple reasons. People in those times didn't have the eating problems we have today—they ate more natural foods and were probably less stressed. Because the Bible is a book designed to be read by all people everywhere, from every culture on earth, you can't set one rule for people's eating habits on such a wide scale. But you can give general guiding principles for healthy eating, and that's what the Bible does. So what are those principles?

The Gospel NOT according to Weightwatchers . . .

Here are a few Bible principles to guide your eating habits:

1. Don't hate yourself

By the time you've passed through puberty, you'll know whether you're going to be tall or short, plump or skinny. No matter what you do, you cannot change your basic shape, the pattern of your weight distribution. Loving yourself is a divine command (Matthew 19:19), and it sure beats the alternative!

2. Don't be obsessed with your looks

Not only is the 'I hate the way I look' mentality a form of inverted pride—because it constantly focuses on poor you—it can also lead to some very unhealthy things, like dieting.

Dieting is actually dangerous for young people—and not much benefit to older people, either. One study found that 30 per cent of Australian women are dieting at any one time. For some teenage girls, the figure climbs to around 42 per cent.[4]

What most of these people don't understand is that 95 per cent of the weight they lose is regained later, according the Royal College of Physicians.[5] When you diet, your body's metabolism slows down so that less fat is burned off. What *is* removed is valuable muscle tissue. You're better off changing your overall eating and exercise habits. Being overly self-conscious has always been a bad idea (Philippians 2:4).

3. Enjoy what you eat

God told the Israelites to celebrate by having feasts several times each year. Food is meant to be enjoyed, not endured (see Proverbs 23:6–7).

4. Share what you eat

Don't flaunt your food in the face of someone else's hunger. Share with those who can't pay you back (Luke 14:12–13).

5. Use meals as social times

Jesus often had great times of fellowship over a meal. In fact, some of His finest ministry was conducted at dinner time (Luke 7:37–50)! Hospitality is a quality the Bible encourages (Romans 12:13).

6. Balance what you eat

I've already shown how the six major food groups are mentioned in the Bible.

7. Don't overdo it

Gluttony demeans human beings, dulling their senses, stripping them of their dignity and leading them to poverty (see Proverbs 23:20–21).

8. Don't become addicted to drink

Alcoholic drink can lull you into a false sense of security and have you thinking you don't need God. Then it becomes the master instead of the servant, and destroys you (see Proverbs 20:1; Isaiah 5:11–12).

9. Fast on occasions

Fasting's not just good for cleaning out the body, it's great for tuning the spiritual ears to hear from God (Ezra 8:23). But it is *never* a good idea for losing weight.

10. Don't condemn others if they don't eat as you do

You may not think eating certain foods or drinking a particular beverage is right. Fine, so don't do it. But don't condemn others Jesus died for, just because you don't like their eating habits (Colossians 2:16–17).

The great beauty rip-off

Is Elle McPherson a perfect '10'? Is she the ultimate beauty? Maybe, but Leonardo Da Vinci wouldn't have thought so. When it came to choosing models for his paintings, he and others of that era would have called on Roseanne before the leggy Ms Elle. To them, thin was *not* in, *fat* was where it's at!

Images of beauty have changed drastically over the centuries. Even today when you travel from country to country you find different ideas on what is considered physically attractive. In strict Muslim countries, for example, men aren't turned on by a woman's legs—they're well and truly covered. Not even the smile is revealed, only the eyes are showing. Guys are turned on by the eyes, or not at all!

And what about the guys? If Arnie the Terminator really is *el perfecto* in the body stakes, how can the rest of us mere mortals ever step out on the beach with pride? Go to any major international art gallery and you won't find many renaissance paintings of men with biceps on their triceps and deltoids on their adenoids! Conan then just wasn't the rage. In fact, many of the most popular guys were kind of pasty-faced, and they wore leggings. (*Can you imagine Rambo a la* AD1500—*in tights and feathered hat?*)

It's sad that most of us never get to appreciate these differences in the way physical attractiveness is measured. If we did, we might not be so hung up about our appearance but be more concerned about what's inside ourselves and other people.

And we don't see what the 'style police' are doing to our brains! These are the ladies and gentlemen of the pop-fashion industry who tell us what we can and can't wear. A member of this force, designer Christian Dior, is reported to have said, 'I consider that without hats, an intrinsic part of fashion, we would have no civilisation.'[6] Oh yes, a man of great depth is Mr Dior!

So many magazines and TV shows foist on us a concept of attractiveness which only a select few in the population will ever get close to matching. Cindi Crawford said, 'Not even I wake up looking like Cindi Crawford!' How many Elles do you actually see gliding around the streets of your town? And who's to say that image of 'good-looking' will last for long anyway?

Pyschologists have now discovered a whole new 'disease' they're calling the *Imagined Ugliness Syndrome*. People who suffer from this perpetually hate what they see in the mirror. They go through life believing they're doomed to be gruesome, even though some of them are quite good looking. They give up on other qualities they possess because they don't look like the person on the cover of *Cosmo* or *Muscle Man!*

Barbie's just a doll

There are thousands of young adults, especially women, for whom the beauty myth is particularly cruel. Many will put themselves through untold misery, malnutrition and sickness to get the Barbie doll figure, and they're not all teenagers.

Bulimia and anorexia are growing problems among young women. A 1983 Sydney University study of women aged fourteen to twenty-five found that 20 to 30 per cent were bulimic or anorexic—most of them bulimic.[7] Studies have shown that the mean age when girls start worrying about their weight is fourteen years and seven months, and the mean age for the onset of dieting and eating disorders is one year after that.

Anorexia (or anorexia nervosa) is characterised by a fear of becoming fat and chronic *under*-eating, which leads to sickness and sometimes death. Some of the other symptoms can be overexercise, laxative abuse, deceitful behaviour to avoid eating, and vomiting. Basically, to be anorexic means to starve yourself. Kaz Cooke writes that, 'Classic anorexics believe they are heading towards the mythical perfect body as demanded by society, and they believe that by controlling their bodies they are controlling their lives.'[8]

Bulimia (or bulimia nervosa) is characterised by *over*-eating, or 'binge-eating', followed by vomiting. This is even more widespread than anorexia. Some experts believe it affects as many as 1 in every 100 girls. Bulimics are often people who are in control of every other area of their lives except this one. Their symptoms can also include fasting, overexercise and the abuse of diet pills and diuretics (drugs which increase the flow of urine). The damage done by both anorexia and bulimia can be irreversible and, yes, fatal.

The two greatest problems with eating disorders like

these is that they so often remain hidden for long periods of time and that they are built around chronically low self-esteem. Those who suffer these conditions will often see small failures as huge disasters. Sadly for these people, the things they make themselves sick for—love and affection—are the very things their condition denies them. One young bulimic woman said, 'I get thin because I think that's what guys want. Then I meet a guy, but as soon as he sees me vomiting, I've lost him.'

Sadly too, it seems society rewards young women for going through all of this. Many models and leading sports women have suffered these conditions in their quest for professional recognition.

If you or a friend of yours is wrestling with a problem of this kind, you can get a referral for expert help from your local doctor, or seek help from one of the specialised support groups now in operation. Whatever you do, don't go to someone who'll tell you it will be OK if you take two aspirin and come back next week!

Is God into beauty?

The Bible says very little about fashion, cosmetics or body mass! The book of Acts does not, for example, say, 'And Paul arrived at Ephesus dressed in a nice little woollen ensemble, in a very daring shade of yellow, with hand-woven tassels around the hem.'

Fashion isn't much talked about in the Bible, because it's not that important to God. Don't ask me what Jesus wore to church, I couldn't tell you. But what I do know is that every notable man and woman in the Bible had an attractive heart.

The Bible says, 'Man looks at the outward appearance, but the Lord looks at the heart' (1 Samuel 16:7). That's *not* to say that how you look is not important at all, because human beings *do* look at our outward appearance—and that is a measure of how we feel about ourselves inside. Fashion design, if that's your interest, is also a great way to express God-given creativity. But you can't *impress* God with your outward appearance—He knows you too well. What does please God is the way we keep the furniture arranged on the *inside.* If we keep the need to please God above the need to impress people, the 'beauty thing' won't be such a stressor.

I remember being rapturously in love with a dark-haired beauty in my high school. Her name was Susan Taylor and on a scale of 1 to 10, she was a 15! Looking back, I hardly remember saying a word to her—she was too gorgeous to talk to—and I guess every guy in our class had a crush on her. But I doubt if any one of us could have told you what her favourite colour was, or what food she liked to eat. We didn't know her at all. Our feelings for her were not based on any assessment of her *character* which is, after all, the thing which will hold you to a person in the long run.

Stressing out . . .

'The evidence of the last two decades has shown that, of all the factors involved, stress is the most significant contributor to disease.'[9]

Yep, it's just as you thought. Your boss *can* make you sick! Even a short stressful event, such as running late for work (or confronting the boss when you get there!) has a real effect on the processes inside your body. Your body simply responds to the demands placed upon it by your brain.

One doctor has written that your brain is not just a computer, it's also an 'apothecary (manufacturer of hundreds of chemical agents and messengers)'.[10] In times of stress this cerebral pharmacy releases three major hormones into your system. The first is *adrenalin,* which pumps glucose into the body and gives you a sudden energy spurt—it gets you ready to fight or flight. The second is *noradrenaline,* which causes your blood pressure to rise and your muscles to go on red alert. The third is *cortisol,* which suppresses the immune system, and makes you more open to that cold you've been avoiding. Too much of this cortisol stuff can cause fats and sugars to clog up your arteries and blood vessels.

OK, so that's what stress can do to the body. *But what exactly is this threatening thing called stress and where does it come from?* Actually stress is not from 'out there', it's from 'in here' within us. It is basically a response we make to certain physical stimuli. Here's how it works. An event occurs which stimulates one or more of our five senses. They send a message to the brain, which then sifts that message through a 'belief system'. Over time we've built up a set of religious, ethical and educational values which shape what we think about our environment. The outward stimulus is given meaning by being filtered through this belief system. Now we know what the stimulus 'means' and we start 'feeling' something about it: joy, depression or even apathy!

These days stress is a major health hazard. It can trigger asthma or it can lead to strokes and coronary heart attacks. How do we combat it? Does God have anything to say on this one? I'm glad you asked because this is the area of health which the Bible has most to comment on. Here are a few of its tips for dealing with stress.

Bible ways to overcome stress

1. Develop a generous spirit

There is something therapeutic about giving to others: giving time, money, encouragement and the benefit of your experience (Acts 20:35: 'It is more blessed to give than to receive'). Giving to others helps you to recognise the good things you possess (Matthew 10:8), and investing in the lives of others does tend to take your mind off your problems. *I can't imagine Mother Teresa needing deep therapy!*

2. Take responsibility

As far as God is concerned, you are not responsible for what other people do to you, or what circumstance throws at you. But you are responsible for how you react to these challenges. You don't have to be helpless or hopeless. In a German POW camp, Victor Frankl realised that although the guards could take away every physical thing he owned and make things tough for him, they could not take away his right to choose how he would react! He could always decide what kind of person he would be. That power was something which could not be stolen from him.

When Judas Iscariot came to betray Jesus with a kiss, the first words Jesus said to him were, 'Friend, do what you came to do' (Matthew 26:50). *Friend!? Surely you're mistaken Jesus!* No, Jesus knew He could not change what Judas had freely chosen to do, but He did have power over His response to it. Don't live with a victim mentality, always blaming everyone else for the way your life has turned out. Decide that you're going to keep control over your own heart (Proverbs 4:23).

3. Practice forgiveness

This relates to the last one. Forgiveness is a decision you make, not a feeling: it's an act of will not whim. Unfortunately, we all have trouble really forgiving, that's why we need to experience deep forgiveness for ourselves. We each need to see our own hurt in proper perspective. Whether you like it or not, it's a fact: you've offended God much more than anyone has ever offended or hurt you. When you feel the deep inner peace that comes from knowing you are forgiven by God, forgiving what others have done to you isn't so hard (Luke 7:40–47).

4. Bring emotions into line with will

Discipline your emotions and mind so that you are not emotion-driven but decision-driven (1 Corinthians 9:27). Learn to talk differently about those who've let you down. Just as there are six major food groups for the body, there are six major food groups for the spirit—prayer, Bible reading, meditating (not the chanting kind, just thinking about or chewing over what you read), fellowship with other like-minded people, sharing your faith and giving. A daily dose of each helps you keep your emotions on a short leash.

5. Trust God

You can learn to trust God with your problem even when it seems outside your control (Psalm 23:4). In fact, it's only when you can no longer manipulate things yourself that you can really trust Him at all!

6. Accept yourself (without neglecting self-improvement!)

In summary, do your best to look and feel healthy; make the most of your natural strengths and improve where you can. All this is honouring God and a sign of self-respect. But don't sacrifice yourself on the altar of physical perfection. *Life's short enough as it is!*

REFERENCES:

1. 'Good as Gold', *Who* magazine, October 24, 1994.
2. Dr. S. I. McMillen, *None Of These Diseases* (Spire Books, 1979), p.65.
3. Tom Peters, *The Tom Peters Seminar* (MacMillan London, 1994), p.108.
4. Kaz Cooke, *Real Gorgeous* (Allen and Unwin, 1994), p.33.
5. Ibid., p.35.
6. Ibid., p.156.
7. Ibid., p.56.
8. Ibid., p.58.
9. 'Can Your Personality Make You Sick?', *Nature and Health* (Vol. 15, No.3, 1994).
10. Keith W. Sehnert, MD, *Selfcare, Wellcare* (Augsburg Pub. House, 1985), p.65.

STUDY GUIDE

Laboratory experiments reveal that very few people care about their apathy on health issues.

Professor Claudius Fritzenbacher III
Emeritus Professor,
Dept. of Verifiable Myths, Camford University.

Warm-ups

What form of exercise are you into at the moment? How many times a week do you do this? For how long? How many times do you eat fast food in a week? Do you feel as if this is doing you good?

Study/Discussion

Look back over the different forms of exercise in this chapter (starting with 'aerobic'). List some specific examples of each type, other than the ones given.

I've quoted a doctor who said, 'The sincere acceptance of the principles and teachings of Christ . . . would at once wipe out more than half the difficulties, diseases and sorrows of the human race.' List some of the teachings of Jesus which would help us become healthier people (in a holistic sense).

Read John 14:1–3; Luke 6:37–38; Philippians 4:4–7. What do you think are some of the points these passages tell us that could help bring down our stress levels?

Barbie *is* just a doll! List some of the qualities you actually *like* about your body. Is there anything you can do to improve some of the areas you don't particularly like? (Don't be too hard on yourself! Remember, even Cindi Crawford doesn't wake up looking like Cindi Crawford!)

Getting Started

Look back over the list of guidelines in this chapter for good eating habits. Which of these could you put into place now to help you eat better?

List some things you can do in the next week to lift your exercise programme to a new level. Now do the same with your 'spiritual exercise programme'.

Further Resources

Mal Fletcher, *Youth: The Endangered Species* (Word Books, 1993), chapter 3 (on drugs).

Film: *The Elephant Man* (about false images of beauty).

Keith W. Sehnert, MD, *Selfcare, Wellcare* (Augsburg Pub. House, 1985).

6

IS GOD MALE?

– FEMINISM AND CHAUVINISM –

*Plato said that a bad man's fate was to be reincarnated
as a woman. Aristotle taught that 'females are imperfect
males'. Josephus the ancient historian held that a
woman is 'inferior to man in every way'. These were
definitely not Sensitive New Age Guys!*

WITH ATTITUDES LIKE this to contend with, is it
any wonder women in modern times have been
looking for a better deal?

In one ancient form of Jewish prayer, a man thanked
God for three things: that he was not a Gentile, a slave, *or
a woman!* In those times women had no legal rights at all.
Even some of the early church fathers blamed women
more than men for the woes of the human race—because
Eve was deceived before Adam (which, by the way, was
also Adam's excuse!)

The feminist movement has achieved some great
things. At times it's been a real force for justice ending
decades, even centuries, of oppression for women. In its
early days some daring female pioneers stood up and were
counted. They gained for women the right to vote and
opened up new career doors. They put the needs and

concerns of women on the political map. How many politicians *don't* talk about women's issues now?

In the sixties, Germaine Greer was a tough-talking street- fighter at the front of a new, fiercer women's movement. Women, wrote Greer, 'were the truly oppressed majority; they should rebel, and withdraw their labour.'[1] Germaine complained that women had value only in the desire they excited in men, rather than in who they were.

In our own time there's still some ground to make up.

Does 'no' ever mean 'yes'?

Mandi Johns was a 30-year-old Australian mother living with a baby daughter and a violent husband. She'd put up with four years of marriage to a guy who was nice at first but then began hitting her. He sometimes forced her to have sex with him. Finally she plucked up the courage to have him charged with assault.

Then she had to sit in court and hear the judge sum up for the jury by saying, 'There is nothing wrong in a husband using "rougher than usual handling" in attempting to have intercourse with his wife.'[2] The jury found the husband innocent, but the judge rightly copped a flogging in the press and in government circles!

'Sexploitation'—exploitation through sex—is still happening in the office too. You know the scene—boss meets pretty female secretary, boss gets too free with his hands or too cheeky with his comments, secretary is under pressure not to lose her job. Once upon a time the woman would say nothing—not any more, Jack. Now there are laws for that kind of thing.

There are other forms of exploitation too. *MIZZ* is a

magazine which targets fourteen- to seventeen-year-old girls in Britain. In one of its school holiday issues, it featured an article about bondage. 'Let's go all the way,' it blared. 'Strange sex! Perversion! Bondage!' It even gave helpful definitions: 'Bondage is the practice of becoming sexually aroused by being tied up.'[3] Call it innocent fun, or 'soft' porn if you like. You can't excuse the fact that this stuff exploits young women because it encourages them to sell themselves out to the *lowest* bidder!

Come on, they're only pictures . . .

Then there's pornography aimed at men. It's a whole industry built around exploiting women, but it also robs guys in the process. According to experts, men who feed on pornography develop a callous attitude towards women. If they get into heavier forms of porn they will gradually look for more and more violent forms to feed on and will even begin to see rape as a trivial offence.[4] Some studies have shown that up to half of the men convicted of rape use 'consenting sex' porn to arouse themselves before finding a victim to attack.[5] In 1985, the FBI found that 81 per cent of the serial killers they interviewed said that their main sexual interest was reading porn.[6]

Porn destroys their whole view of the dignity of women, and their view of relationships—some studies show that porn makes being faithful in a relationship seem less appealing to men.[7]

Men also become less sensitive to the effect this stuff has on them. Porn can actually have an addictive effect—one sexually arousing experience can cause craving for another because of the way sexual fantasies attach themselves to the brain. Some men get so hooked on the 'high', they lose the line between fantasy and reality and begin living out what they read. (See *'Youth: The Endangered Species'*, pp.39–41)

Hugh Heffner, the 'pioneer' behind *Playboy* magazine, was once asked whether he'd like his daughter to pose nude for a magazine like his. He thought about it and then gruffly replied, 'No!' He knew what *Playboy* pictures do to men's minds and he didn't want his daughter to be on the receiving end of all that drooling lust. Shame he didn't feel that way about other people's daughters!

Porn's not just about 'naughty pictures'—*porn's about ruined lives, on both sides of the gender fence.*

And then there were none (men, that is) . . .

There's another kind of exploitation going on too. It's a strange form of reverse discrimination. One guy called me on talk-back radio to complain that, as a bouncer at a nightclub, he was being harassed by women who were getting too free with their hands. He felt powerless to do anything about it because he knew—and so did they—that if he really objected he'd lose his job. It seems being treated like a piece of meat was part of the job description. (Anything to keep the punters happy!)

There is a radical fringe to the feminist movement which would like to see injustice continue—*but this time against men.* Men are, after all, exploiters of women. Men should become the weaker sex, the downtrodden masses. Men should lose most or all of their authority—in the home, in business, in government. Men should get out of the way so that women can run the world, the right way.

Yes it's only a fringe, the group who feel this way, but it is out there. It's made up of women who've been hurt, women who are angry, women who can't, or won't, forgive. Women who've given up on men altogether. Women who want the tables turned. They're calling for androgyny—the breaking down of all differences between male and female. They don't just want the sexes to be equal, *they want them to be identical.*

Of course, if you can mix these strong feelings with a little religious zeal, you're on your way to changing the way the world thinks. Enter the 'ecofeminist' movement. If you mix some ancient Eastern goddess religion—from Hinduism, for example—together with some pagan Earth Mother religion which sees the Earth as a living, female being, you're moving towards the dawning of the age of Aquarius!

Ecofeminism marries New Age, Shirley MacLaine spirituality with the feminist cause. Believers see our planet as having all the characteristics of a strong and fertile mother. She wants to nurture and protect her natural order and her offspring, including human beings. Unfortunately people, especially men, keep screwing things up and throwing things out of kilter, so good ol' Mother Earth has to let off steam through earthquakes, tidal waves and the like to bring things back into balance. The Christian church is just part of an outdated system which has oppressed women through its teaching about a harsh male 'sky-god'. There's even a fringe to this fringe group who say that women should be reinstated as 'holy prostitutes', *so that a woman's body becomes something 'sacred' again!*

OK, so what alternative does the Bible offer?

I'm glad you asked. The Bible has a lot to say about the roles of men and women, and it's not as old-fashioned as you may think! Some people make the mistake of assuming that everything that's 'old' must also be 'Bible'. Untrue. As we'll see, this book has often challenged the status quo on the subject of the equality of the sexes (and it still does!)

The Bible says there are three key events in our history which have shaped the way men and women relate to each other. First there's the *Creation*. Good news, *you're not a monkey who got lucky!* You're a designer model. Some people will tell you that you started out 'a little lower than a tadpole'; the Bible says God made us 'a little lower than the angels'. As one old preacher said, 'You can pray to your father up a tree . . . I'll pray to my Father up in heaven!' *Yessir!*

At Creation, writes John Stott, we were given three things—equality, dignity and responsibility.[8] Genesis tells us that God made human beings in His image, or after His likeness, and He specifically made them male and female (Genesis 1:26–27). Throughout the Bible, women are spoken of as representing part of the image of God. They are not God's great afterthought—'Hey, how are these Adam guys going to reproduce?' Women are part of the image of God.

There are many scriptures, especially in the Old Testament, which actually speak of God in feminine terms. *They what?!* They use feminine word-pictures to describe God's nature. Here's a sample:

— God is like a midwife who brings us out of our mother's womb (Psalm 22:9);

— God is like a loving mother who breast-feeds her children to comfort them (Psalm 131:2);

— God is like a merciful 'master' and a 'mistress' to us (Psalm 123:2);

— God is like a mother who doesn't forget her children (Isaiah 49:13–15);

— God is like a woman in childbirth who cries out for those she loves (Isaiah 42:14);

— God is like a woman who loses her best coin and looks for it through the house (Luke 15: 8–10).

There is something in the nature of God which seems to link up with both the masculine and feminine in His creation. *So why does the Bible still call God a 'He'?* Because that's the way God has chosen to be known. It's OK to change words in the Bible like 'man' to 'mankind', and 'brethren' to 'sister and brothers', as many modern translations are doing. After all, that's what the original writers meant. But Jesus calls God 'Father', not 'Mother' and Himself the 'Son', not 'Child' of God. Some things, it seems, are not negotiable!

Does that mean women are inferior to men? Ask my wife if she's inferior to me. (She's Welsh, she'll certainly tell you straight out!) We are each strong in some areas and weak in others. Where I have a weakness Davina will have a strength. That's what makes our marriage work, and that's how God meant us to relate to each other. At creation Eve was not a plaything for Adam ('Here Adam, have a new toy . . . '). No, she was absolutely essential to his life on Planet Earth. Without her he could not have survived and creation would have been incomplete. God said: 'It is not good for man to be alone' (Genesis 2:18).

But doesn't the Bible say Eve was made as a 'Helper' for Adam? Yes it does, in Genesis 2:18, but that same word is used many other times in the Old Testament and in most cases it is used of God Himself! (For example: Genesis 49:25; Exodus 18:4; Deuteronomy 33:26; 1 Samuel 7:12.) It's not meant to be a put-down, but a term reflecting the dignity of woman. It means that the woman 'completes' the man.

So at creation man and woman were given *dignity*— they were like God, in a way the animals were not—and *equality*—neither one was more important in God's eyes. But they were *not* made identical. In fact, they could not complement each other if they were identical.

General Eva Burrows is a woman who rose to become the head of a huge world-wide organisation called the Salvation Army. She is a success in her own field, a world leader. She says, 'To be an equal does not mean you have to be the same.'[9] The Bishop of Paris in AD 1157 put it this way, 'Eve was not taken from the feet of Adam to be his slave, nor from his head to be his lord, but from his side to be his partner.'[10]

So why aren't things so rosy now?

The second key event the Bible talks about is the *Fall*. Creation, it says, has been distorted by man's moral disobedience of God. There's a law in this universe of ours—you sow carrot seeds and you'll reap carrots. What we sow we reap; what goes around comes around. It works that way in the moral sphere too.

Adam and Eve made the wrong choices. They chose

to take a short-cut in their own personal development plan. They wanted to be 'like God', and they wanted promotion quickly. Tragedy struck in their relationship to each other. Alienation and mistrust crept in; mis-understanding and bitterness became part of their life together. They started having 'domestics'!

It seems the Fall affected males and females differently. One writer has said that man's first sin towards woman, even today, is 'trying to exercise dominion without regard to God's original plan for male/female relation-ships'.[11] His natural drive to be a leader is twisted into a desire to dominate. The woman's sin, on the other hand, is to 'use the preservation of . . . relationships as an excuse not to exercise accountable dominion in the first place'.[12] Her God-given talent for preserving and nurturing relationships is bent into a 'keep the family together, no matter what he does to us' mentality. Both are wrong because that's not how God created things to be. Both come from the Fall, not the Creation.

Will things ever change?

The third great shaping event in history according to the Bible is called *Redemption*. Redemption is God buying us back from slavery to a fallen way of life. It is God paying the price for our freedom. That price was the greatest which could ever be paid—the life of His Son, Jesus Christ.

Redemption is the cure for the effects of the Fall. It recovers for us what was lost from the original Creation. The Bible says that we're not going to see a full recovery until Jesus returns and God makes a new heaven and new earth. But we can have a little taste of God's kingdom in the here and now. In fact, Christians are commanded to live in a way which points forward to that higher kingdom. The Holy Spirit comes to help the Christian enjoy the benefits of a new life through what Jesus did on the cross. That will include having a renewed appreciation for the roles of men and women in God's plan.

So things will change. One day the kingdoms of this earth will become God's kingdom again, as they were in the beginning. Until then, the Spirit of God is here on earth working through the church to point societies back to God's right way of doing things. But what's the standard God is pointing us to? What is His intention for women and men?

Jesus: women's libber!

What?! Jesus in the ranks of the feminists? *Jesus marching in the picket lines waving a 'Sisterhood' banner?!* No, not quite. But Jesus was a liberator of women, in the truest sense of the world. For Him, freeing women to their God-given potential was not just some popular cause for which to fight (it wasn't a cause at all in those days). Nor was it a political platform to win votes. It was part of His mission and He was passionate about it.

There is one great statement Jesus made right at the beginning of His public ministry which shows us His real heart:

'The Spirit of the Lord is on me,
because he has anointed me
to preach good news to the poor.
He has sent me to proclaim freedom
for the prisoners

and recovery of sight for the blind,
to release the oppressed,
to proclaim the year of the Lord's favour.'
(Luke 4:18–19)

What did he say? *'To release the oppressed.'* You have to say that women at the time of Jesus were among the world's oppressed. In Old Testament Israel, the family patriarch was the absolute ruler of his household and clan. Women were basically the property of their husbands—although many male characters in the Bible treated their wives with more respect than that. The prophets, however, looked forward to a brighter day, a new kingdom where right-eousness ruled, where the downtrodden classes were given justice at last.

Jesus saw the fulfilment of that prophetic hope as His personal mission on earth. Right from the start of His life story we see a departure from the common attitude towards women at the time. Mary His mother was called 'blessed among women' and was recognised as someone to be highly honoured. When Jesus went out to teach and preach He actually *encouraged* women to learn from Him. And women just weren't supposed to learn *anything!*

'I am woman, watch me learn!'

Barbra Streisand directed and starred in the film *Yentl*, a musical drama set in the nineteenth century. It's about a young Jewess whose greatest desire in life is to study the Jewish religion and philosophy. She lives within a very structured social network where women studying at that level, well, it was just not done! So to hit the books and attend the lectures, Yentl resorts to dressing and living as a man.

Jesus lived in the same atmosphere. Back in Jesus' day some teachers said it would be better to burn the Jewish Law books than to let women study them!

Martha, whose brother Lazarus Jesus brought back from the grave, complained one day of her sister Mary who was sitting at Jesus' feet listening to Him teach (Luke 10). 'Hey, Jesus,' she grumbled, 'Why don't you tell Mary to get her act together. She should be out here in the kitchen helping me with the women's work.' What was Jesus' response? He could have screamed, 'OK boys, who let this *woman* into My lecture?' But He didn't. He said, 'Martha, Mary has chosen the better way to occupy her time. I can't tell her off for wanting to learn'. The inference here is, 'Martha, why don't you take a leaf out of your sister's book?'

Then there was the woman Jesus met on His way through Samaria (John 4). For Jesus just to go through this part of the country was radical. There was racial conflict between Jews and the Samaritans.

Jews considered them half-castes, 'cross-breeders' with pagan cultures, an insult to the purity of the Jewish race. So on his way through this 'no go' area Jesus meets and strikes up a long conversation with a woman who is out drawing water from the town well. Nothing unusual in that, you say—men speak with women every day of the week.

Yes, they do nowadays, but not back then. It was not considered proper for a Jewish male to speak with any woman on the street, *even if she was his wife!* Also, this woman was an outcast, a 'brazen hussie'. She was the friendly neighbourhood home-wrecker. She'd been through five husbands and the man she was living with now was not her husband. Nobody wanted to know her—not even in her own town. That's why she was out doing the chores in the heat of the day, when all the other sensible women were indoors, watching Oprah Winfrey or something.

What does Jesus *see* in this woman? Her need—the deep, painful longing for real acceptance and forgiveness. In one conversation He brings her to a life-changing faith in God, then she brings half her village to the same conviction. Not a bad afternoon's work, Jesus! *Again, He breaks with tradition where a woman in need is concerned.*

There are many other stories in the Gospels of how Jesus met the needs of women. Some came for healing, others for the deliverance of a loved one. Some were even too afraid to ask for anything, but they got it anyway (see Matthew 9:20–21)! Jewish women had never seen a teacher like this One. He didn't just say nice things about them in private, He helped them in public.

Jesus did a lot for His women friends and colleagues, and they were devoted to Him because of it. Women were among the major financial supporters of His ministry. And women were key figures at the two major, crowning events of Jesus' life—the cross and the resurrection. Some of His female followers were among the only people who stuck by Him during His coldest hours. They stood near His cross, mourning His death—which is something most of His gentlemen friends were too afraid to do. They were the ones who prepared His body for burial, long after the men had gone into hiding. And they were the ones He appeared to first when He was miraculously raised from the dead on the third day.

The author of John's Gospel says that Jesus did many other works than those recorded in his book, and that if all his good works were written, probably the world couldn't contain the books written (John 21:25). I can't help feeling that many of those books would be *packed* with stories about how Jesus blessed women.

'Without fuss or publicity,' writes John Stott, 'Jesus terminated the curse of the Fall, reinvested woman with her partially lost nobility and reclaimed for His new kingdom community the original creation blessing of sexual equality.'[13]

Isn't the church anti-women?

People often confuse Victorian values with Bible values. They think that if women in respectable, church-going, nineteenth-century society were not encouraged to develop their gifts, the Bible must discourage women's freedom. *Wrong!*

Sure, the established Christian church had more influence on Western society back then, but the church was often filled with the kind of stuffy, class-conscious respectability which even Jesus had great problems with! Jesus hated the tight-fisted, narrow-minded religiosity of religious people in His time. He called the moralisers of His own day 'white-washed tombs' and 'snakes', because they looked down their noses at everyone else, as if they were morally superior beings. The Pharisees would have fitted well into the 'high society' of the last century.

Even in our own time, the historic churches have

sometimes been slow to recognise the true potential of their women. In some parts of the world the only thing you ever read about the church is that they haven't yet decided whether or not to allow women into the priesthood. That's sad, because it reflects a narrow view of what the New Testament says about the roles of women and men.

Paul wrote a good deal about the place of the sexes in his letters of advice to the early churches. In his letter to the Galatians, for example, he says that in the church, 'There is neither Jew nor Greek, slave nor free, *male nor female,* for you are all one in Christ Jesus' (Galatians 3:28).

Does that mean that for Christians there are supposed to be no differences between men and women? Of course not. Jews would always be Jews, Greeks would always be Greeks, and boys would always be boys. The point he's making is that Greeks were once considered second-class citizens because only Jews possessed God's Law. Now, because of the cross, God has given Greeks the same status as Jews—they're both saved only by faith in Jesus. It's the same with men and women, He says. They both have equal standing. In God's kingdom, women are not second class citizens.

OK, so men and women are equal in status before God. But what does that mean in practical terms? *Doesn't Paul say that a man is 'the head' of his wife?* Yes he does (Ephesians 5:23), but we need to see what he means by those words, not what *we think* he means.

In ancient culture the head was not thought of as it is today—the engine room of the whole body, the place where the brain barks out orders for the rest of the anatomy to obey! The head was thought of as the part of the body which nurtured, or fed, the rest. The head integrated and held the body together. So Paul says that a man is responsible for nurturing his wife, for protecting her, for seeing her fulfil her real call.

He says basically the same thing in his letter to the Ephesians:

> Husbands, love your wives, just as Christ loved the church and gave himself up for her . . . In this same way, husbands ought to love their wives *as their own bodies.* He who loves his wife loves himself. After all, no one ever hated his own body, *but he feeds and cares for it,* just as Christ does the church . . .
> (Ephesians 5:25,28,29, emphases added)

Here men are commanded to show their wives the same unselfish, releasing love Jesus showed the church. How can that be a put-down for women? In the light of Paul's culture, it was a big step *up* for them.

What's all this talk about 'submission' then?

Aren't women told to submit to men? Doesn't that mean they're doormats again? No. In the Bible there is a pattern given for how people should relate to each other. You can't have real freedom in any group of people without order. There has to be some kind of common understanding as to who does what, or there's chaos. While woman is given a very special place in the home and the church, it is not the same as man's place.

In Paul's writings, men are to give a lead in the home, to set a standard for others to copy in the way they live. *It's all about leadership, not dictatorship.* The man is to earn the respect of his wife, who should have a submissive attitude towards her man. But we need to define 'submission'. One female writer puts it beautifully, '[Submission is] voluntary yielding in love . . . It is a gift a wife offers her husband, not a right the husband can ever demand of his wife.'[14] *Submission is the attitude of wanting to please someone, and being willing to yield in love (not fear).*

What about leadership positions in the church? *Doesn't Paul say that women should be 'silent' in church, that they're not allowed to teach?* (See 1 Corinthians 14:33–36.) There's been some real debate among good Christian people on this one. There'll probably always be some disagreement about how to interpret what Paul is on about. Basically though, I think Paul is saying that women in the church at Corinth need to respect the fact that church gatherings should be orderly affairs. That's the whole reason he's writing this chapter—to men as well as women (verse 40). There shouldn't be chatter going on in the background, or women eagerly asking their husbands questions about the teaching. They should do that at home, he says (verse 35). He's already said that when the Christians come together 'everyone' will have a hymn, a word of encouragement or a spiritual utterance to share (verse 26). When I last read my dictionary, 'everyone' included women.

There is another place where Paul mentions leadership (1 Timothy 2:11–15), but many leading scholars believe that this refers to women usurping a man's role— teaching with an attitude problem. It's not so much about women teaching as it is about women snatching the man's role.[15]

And what about women being 'the weaker sex'—doesn't that line come from the Bible? Sure does (1 Peter 3:7). Generally speaking it is true that men are capable of physically heavier work than women. Even most feminists have no trouble with this. (Although boys, on average, are more fragile at birth than girls!) Actually, this verse is aimed at men, not women. It is commanding men to protect their wives, who share equal partnership with them in the faith.

But think about it this way too—what many women may lack in areas of physical strength in comparison with men, they well and truly make up in emotional strength. We guys could learn a lot from our sisters when it comes to being open and vulnerable. If that's part of this 'weakness' women have, I say, *give us more weakness*!

It's all about attitude . . .

In the New Testament we have the beautiful picture of the sexes Paul Stookey spoke about in his *Wedding Song*: 'Woman draws her life from man and gives it back again.' Neither man nor woman are independent of each other. They are *interdependent*—they need each other, they complement each other. That's how they were made to be. They shouldn't threaten each other or fight over whose turf is what—they shouldn't need to.

In her book about women's roles, Joan Martin says that Christian women should not 'go to extremes, but rather take the "radical middle" '.[16] She continues, 'rebellion and hatred will never bring in the kingdom of God . . . I believe God wants an alternative society where men and women together, bearing the image of God, show forth redemption.'[17]

As for us men, we should not allow women to be

oppressed by anyone for any reason, if it is within our power to change things. We should treat our sisters with respect for the dignity God gave them in Eden. We must learn to encourage them to reach their full potential for His glory, without being patronising *or* threatened by their successes.

The final word here should go to Jesus Himself. He paid a greater price than any other person to liberate both men and women. He said, 'So in everything, do to others what you would have them do to you' (Matthew 7:12).

Hey, if we live by that creed, we won't find getting along with each other is as difficult as we may think.

REFERENCES:

1. Quoted by John Stott, *Issues Facing Christians Today* (Marshall Pickering, 1984), p.256.
2. 'Picking Up the Pieces', *WHO* magazine (May 17, 1993).
3. Quoted by Dave and Anne Carlos, *Care For The Family* (Issue 4, 1993).
4. Dr Jerry R. Kirk, *The Power of the Picture* (Focus on the Family, 1990), p.8.
5. Ibid., p.6, quoting report for Canadian Department of Justice.
6. Ibid., p.6.
7. Ibid., p.8.
8. John Stott, op. cit., pp.155–160.
9. Quoted by Joan Martin, *The Ladies Aren't For Silence,* (Word Books, 1991), p.60.
10. Quoted by John Stott, ibid., p.264.

11. Mary Stewart van Leeuwen, *Gender and Grace: Women and Men in a Changing World* (Inter-Varsity Press, 1990), p.46.
12. Ibid.
13. John Stott, op. cit., p.261.
14. Valerie Griffiths, in *The Ladies Aren't for Silence*, op. cit., p.75.
15. Joan Martin, op. cit.
16. Ibid., p.64.
17. Ibid., pp.67–68.

STUDY GUIDE

Clinical studies have proven that 50 per cent of the population are seriously lacking in male hormones . . . and proud of it!

Professor Claudius Fritzenbacher III
Emeritus Professor,
Dept. of Verifiable Myths, Camford University.

Warm-ups

What are some ways in which you think society discriminates against women? What are some ways it discriminates against men? What do you think are the top three issues concerning sexual discrimination or 'sexploitation' in society today (which three need to be addressed first)?

Study/Discussion

Which are the three key events the Bible says have shaped how men and women relate to each other?

Read Genesis 1:26–28; 2:18–25. I've said that, at Creation, God gave us equality and dignity. What do you think each of these means in terms of gender roles?

The nature of man- and womanhood was changed by the Fall. What did men lose (how was their attitude to women affected by this), and what did women lose?

Read Luke 10:38–42. Discuss what this has to say about Jesus' attitude to gender roles and stereotypes.

Read Ephesians 5:22–29. How should a husband view his wife (and vice versa)?

Getting Started

Look at your current work/family/life situation. How can you become active in changing sexual stereotypes where you are right now?

Further Resources

Film: *Yentl*, starring Barbra Streisand. (A young woman's efforts to overcome stereotypes).

John Stott, *Issues Facing Christians Today* (Marshall Pickering, 1984).

7

IS GAY OK?

'I'm not gay . . . I'm normal!' So said a minister on radio. Provocative, sure—but how accurate is a statement like that? What is God's attitude to homosexuality and homosexuals? Are people born homosexual, and if they are, how do you know if you are gay?

Let's get the words right

Homophile: Some people, even noted Christian authors like Francis Schaeffer, have believed that there are men and women who are born with a natural tendency towards affection for the same sex. 'Not all homophiles,' says Schaeffer, 'practise homosexuality.'[1] In fact, these people would be in the minority among practising homosexuals.

Homosexual: A person who habitually takes part in sexual acts with another (or others) of the same sex. These acts have become part of—perhaps the centre of—their lifestyle. Lesbians are female homosexuals. Francis Schaeffer writes, 'Not all those who practise homosexuality were born homophiles.'[2]

Lobbyist: A person whose job is to influence politicians

in the making of laws which favour a certain (usually minority) group.

Heterosexual: A person who practises the sexual act with another (or others) of the opposite sex.

Gay: A word coined and used by some homosexuals to describe their way of life. To be gay, for many homosexuals, is to become part of a social network which gives them an identity in the community and supports them in their lifestyle.

Homophobia: Originally meaning an irrational fear of homosexuals. This term has been stretched by gay lobbyists to include any belief system which does not completely line up with theirs! For them, it is equal to 'bigotry'.

The gay lobby

Before we look at homosexuality itself—and the needs of homosexuals—we need to understand the people who make the most noise on this subject, the gay lobbyists. These are the men and women who manipulate with such skill much of the information we're given about homosexuality through the media.

First, we need to understand that these lobbyists do *not* speak with authority for all practising homosexuals! In fact, in some places homosexuals feel embarrassment and frustration at some of the actions of these groups. And more than a few homosexuals are anything *but* 'gay' (happy) about the lifestyle they're into.

The aim of most gay lobbyists is to take homosexuality from being seen as a detestable practice spurned by society, to being acceptable and even desirable. A leading homosexual magazine in America published an article which outlines several strategies designed to change society. One strategy involved 'desensitisation', or helping the public to 'view homosexuality with indifference'. Another required that homosexuals be portrayed as victims, so that the rest of the population would assume the role of sympathetic protector. A third idea involved making those who openly oppose homosexuality look like 'ranting homophobes', linking them with extremist groups like the Klu Klux Klan.[3]

When you read the newspapers these days you see how successful these strategies have already been. In some places homosexuals are already enjoying protection in law as a minority group, and receiving privileges normally reserved for people who suffer, for example, as a result of racism. The AIDS crisis, though certainly an international tragedy, is being cleverly used by some lobbyists to gain sympathy for the homosexual lifestyle.

One of the largest lobby groups is ACT-UP (the letters stand for 'AIDS Coalition To Unleash Power'). According to one observer, this organisation is 'hell-bent on the utter and complete annihilation of society—at least as we know it.'[4] I saw a TV interview involving a prominent Canadian lesbian activist. She said, 'I think we face a need to re-invent the world. A lesbian who doesn't is an endangered lesbian.'

The power of lobby groups to influence governments is based on their ability to get people demonstrating on the streets! There's nothing like repeated TV pictures of dissatisfied people marching the streets to get things moving at the town hall.

Not only do groups like this try to influence lawmakers (often through intimidation), they also work to spread their beliefs by changing the English language. Homosexuals are called 'gays'—a word which is meant to show them as happy, carefree, liberated people. The rest of us are 'straight'—that is, we're boring, strictly uncool, all locked up in our restrictive lifestyle. I have a great empathy for the needs of the homosexual—which we'll look at shortly—but I refuse to call myself 'straight'. It's a term that's meant to be pejorative, a put-down. That's reverse discrimination!

Sinclair Rogers (Sy to his friends) is a counsellor and speaker on sex issues. He calls himself a 'recovered homosexual' and runs an organisation called Choices, which is devoted to providing counselling and support services for homosexual people who want 'out' (not out of the closet, out of the lifestyle!). Sy says,

> These days many people are tripping over themselves to avoid being perceived as 'discriminatory' and 'insensitive' . . . Yet many gay activists, dissatisfied with even this, have broadened the definition of 'homophobia' . . . [to] include those who dare to disagree with pro-gay perspective and philosophy. Either you're completely pro-gay and therefore 'enlightened and progressive' or they label you a backward 'bigoted homophobe'.[5]

Rage!

That's the only word to describe what motivates some of these outspoken activists. They strike out in anger against anyone who tries to 'repress' them with ideas they don't like. It's natural that the church will be in their sights, because for them it represents ideas they hate.

Here's what an ACT-UP spokesperson had to say

about the church: 'We have just come out and in so doing have exposed the mean-spirited nature of Judaeo-Christian morality. You have been narrow-minded and self-righteous . . . we are going to force you to recant everything you have believed or said about sexuality.'[6]

Is that intimidation, or what? Either you voluntarily change to suit us, they're saying, or we'll force you to do so. When a church leader in San Francisco tried to make a peaceful stand against the rise of gay power in his community, he was mocked in the media, he had his house fire-bombed at night and members of his church were constantly harassed as they went about their daily lives. He also received many death threats.[7]

A leading American homosexual magazine made this 'prophecy' to the church. 'You will instruct your young people in homosexual as well as heterosexual behaviour and you will go out of your way to make certain that homosexual youths are allowed to date.' What's more, the article claimed, 'We will . . . want to expunge a number of passages from your scriptures and rewrite others.'[8]

Them's fighting words! *All the while, they're demanding that everyone else be more tolerant and show more understanding!*

OK, so that's the lobbyists, but what about the average person who is involved with a homosexual lifestyle? Are they justified in pursuing their sexual habits? There are several issues we need to look at here, and I'll put them as questions. Read on . . .

Is homosexuality normal for some people?

How do people first become involved in homosexuality? Are they born with genes that prefer the same sex? Where does it all begin, in their nature or their nurture, the way they were raised? The personal story of Sy Rogers isn't an unusual one.

> The first half of my life was an emotional concentration camp. My alcoholic mother was killed in a car wreck when I was four. Prior to that, I was sexually molested by a family 'friend'. After my mum's death, I was separated from my father for a year. I lived in an emotional vacuum. My identity and security as a male was left unaffirmed and un-nourished . . .

Sy goes on to describe his early years in school where he was constantly put down because of his effeminate mannerisms. He was labelled a homosexual by other kids, and a failure as a man. He felt attraction to members of the same sex, and with it shame and fear.

He continues, 'A few years later, when eventually involving myself in the gay scene, I felt such a sense of relief. I felt accepted and understood. At last, I had a place to belong. It was great for a while.'

He was living in Hawaii and his two homosexual room-mates became the first men 'married' in that state's first non-official gay wedding. Later, though, they told him that they were 'overcoming' homosexuality, that God was helping them and that they were praying for him. OK, Sy, it's back to you . . .

> My own journey out of the gay life first began with my attempt at securing love by becoming a woman through a sex change. Though I did not get around to ever having the surgery, I was on hormone therapy and lived as a woman for about a year-and-a-half. Yet, even then I

realised that surgery couldn't really solve my problems and wouldn't secure love for me.'[9]

We'll come back to Sy's story later. As a counsellor, he says he hears similar stories many times over. He claims that of his homosexually orientated clients in 1991, 83 per cent of the men and almost 70 per cent of the women reported that they were sexually abused or molested before the age of twelve. Well over 90 per cent said that they felt neglected or unloved as children, especially by the parent of the same sex.[10]

At present there is *no* scientific research into how either the brain or the genes work which proves conclusively that people can be born 'gay'. Of course, even if science does come up with something along those lines, it wouldn't mean that every homosexual is influenced by it, or that people who are influenced will have to behave as homosexuals.

So where does homosexual inclination come from? Well, it's hard to make statements which are true for every single person, but experts are able to make some generalisations based on their client histories.

'I agree with many professionals,' says Rogers, 'who view stereotypical homosexuality as a symptom of arrested emotional and gender identity development.'[11] *'Run that by me again!'*, you say. OK, some types of homosexuality are the result of problems in the psychological development of a person. Children who do not develop a natural bond with parents, especially the same-sex parent, feel a 'love deficit', a hunger for security. This love from the same-sex parent is especially important between the ages of four and fourteen years. Without it the child's sense of what it means to be male or female will not develop properly. He or she will compensate for what is missing, usually by focusing away from the same-sex parent to same-sex peers.

Over time, a 'same-sex fixation' develops and this dependence becomes sexualised during puberty—or even earlier, if a child is affected by abuse. Most people feel some *temporary* same-sex infatuation of some kind during their teen years—that does *not* make them homosexual!

Rogers reminds us that, 'Ultimately homosexuality is not so much about "love" or "sex". It's about need.'[12] If you listen to the rhetoric of homosexual lobbyists, you'll often hear the pain of rejection coming through. In many cases people became involved in this lifestyle because of rejection, and now they suffer more rejection because of it. That drives them further into the gay scene, where they find some degree of support.

We should remember, of course, that we all have flaws in our sexuality. We are all fallen creatures in one way or another. We may not have acted out all of our fantasies, but we've certainly each had our share of lustful thoughts, none of which are really pleasing to our Maker. With that in mind, John Stott says, 'we have no right to dehumanise' those who engage in homosexual practices, to treat them like lepers or monsters from an alien planet.[13] In all our dealings we should certainly 'speak the truth', but do it 'with the accent of love' (Ephesians 4:15, Barclay's translation).

Surely that many (homosexual) people can't be wrong?

This sounds like a convincing argument at first. If a lot of people want to live this way, how can it be wrong? Of course, having sheer numbers in favour of something doesn't make that something morally right. We'll look at morality in a moment. But first let's get one thing clear: there are not as many practising homosexuals in the community as you've been lead to believe. Some lobbyists will tell you that homosexuals represent a decent chunk of society and that their numbers are growing all the time.

One man who did a great deal to help this argument along was Dr Alfred Kinsey. His 'research' into the sexuality of men and women (and children) has given supporters of 'new morality' a platform of scientific-sounding facts, figures and jargon to build on. People who like the idea of 'sexual liberation' cling to his teachings as if they come from some kind of 'Bible'. In his 1948 *Male Report* Kinsey claimed that:

- 85 per cent of males in the US have intercourse prior to marriage
- nearly 70 per cent of men have sex with prostitutes
- 30–40 per cent of husbands have intercourse outside marriage
- 37 per cent of all males have homosexual experiences between their teen years and old age.[14]

That last one is the 'doozey'! Over one third of all men, he says, become involved with some kind of homosexual activity in their adult years. Gay lobbyists have used the work of people like Kinsey, in justifying their claims that around 10 per cent of the male population in developed countries are practising homosexuals.

In a very recent study, which is even more extensive than Kinsey's, the number of active male homosexuals in America was just 2.7 per cent of the population (1.2 per cent for women)![15]

Unfortunately for 'sexual liberationists', Kinsey's work is now questioned by many leading researchers, for two reasons. Firstly, because the samples of people he interviewed for his studies did not represent the bulk of the population. For example, there were many paedophiles, exhibitionists and prison inmates included. He loaded his samples with people he thought would help him come up with the result he happened to like. Secondly, because his research claimed that adult-child sexual activity did not necessarily do the child any harm. He seemed to think that it could do the child some *good*, helping it to feel loved and secure![16] Hey, are you listening? *Do you know anyone who was abused as a child and who now thinks it was helpful to them?!* Get real Dr Kinsey!

What is also disturbing to many modern social scientists is the way Kinsey got his 'facts'. Some say that many of the things he did to children during his research— his experiments—were nothing short of criminal.[17]

But you can't legislate morality— can you?

Again, this sounds convincing. If adults choose to do something, how can anyone else stop them? Actually, I missed a phrase, didn't I? That's right—'if they're not hurting anybody'. We think that's a very convenient line because it means we don't have to include child molesters or rapists in our argument. Actually, there are those who in all seriousness advocate that child sexual activity is quite normal; that just as some people are born homosexual, others are born with a 'taste' for having sex with children.

One active paedophile, and leader of a world organisation promoting sex with children, wrote the following: 'Perhaps the most striking of the Kinsey findings, as they concerned pre-adolescent children, relates to their capacity for sexual orgasm.'[18] Presumably, this would be his defence for having sex with children—it's OK because it's physically possible!

One leading 'sexologist' in the USA is Dr Mary S. Calderone. Here's what this leading 'authority' in her field had to say about child-sex, 'If the child really enjoys [sexual relationship with an adult] it may be the only time the child ever gets a loving touch.' She says children can actually find these relationships 'warm and seductive'.[19] *Hey Doc, stay away from my kids!*

You just can't argue that certain behaviours are acceptable simply because 'nobody gets hurt'. Who judges whether anybody gets hurt? Does the self-confessed child-molester mentioned above? Or the doctor who says children benefit from sexual acts with adults? Then who? If you build your morality on this kind of thinking, you're on very shaky ground.

Also, there is now available overwhelming medical evidence which shows that homosexuals *are* in fact hurting someone—themselves and their partners. Consider these facts:

— the average age at death for homosexual men (who don't die of AIDS) is forty-two years (forty-nine for lesbians). The average age of death from AIDS is thirty-nine years for men.

— the average age at death for other men in the population is seventy-five years (seventy-nine for women)

— male homosexuals are fourteen times more likely to catch syphilis than other men and eight times more likely to catch hepatitis A or B.[20]

Some authorities believe that health problems among active homosexuals are caused by two factors. The first is the sheer physical abuse of this type of sexual activity—when alien objects and substances are forced into internal organs, it doesn't do the anatomy a lot of good. The second fact, backed up by research, is that gay males in particular are much less likely to remain faithful to one partner for long. In some of these relationships, 'affairs' are seen as desirable.

Does all this sound to you as if nobody is getting hurt? Should we let people kill themselves slowly, just because they want to do it? *Without at least saying something's wrong, and trying to help them?!*

But if you relax standards, some may ask, and let homosexuals do as they please, wouldn't that mean they'll be less promiscuous? Maybe they'll clean up their act a bit. History has shown that whenever society relaxes its standards, it becomes more promiscuous in behaviour. The social fabric begins to break up. In cities like New York and San Francisco, where homosexuals have been recognised with all kinds of special privileges, the promiscuity among them hasn't really changed at all.

Can you legislate morality? Of course you can. *It's the only thing you can legislate!* That's what laws are—written codes which reflect moral standards. Laws ensure that the immorality of the few is not forced on the majority. The homosexual lobby is on about morals as much as anyone else, though they might not like to admit it. The real question is not 'Should we legislate morality?' but *'Whose* morality should we legislate?' Whose morality should we call normal and best? Judaeo-Christian morality, which has held our civilisation together for thousands of years— or that of the radical few, some of whom are slowly, sadly killing themselves and each other?

What does the Bible say about homosexuality?

There are some modern social issues the Bible says nothing about directly. In some cases, we are guided more by the principles of the Bible than by specific commands. But the the Bible *does* specifically mention homosexuality a number of times, and each time we are warned to avoid this kind of lifestyle.

Let me note here that not everything church people say is necessarily from the teachings of the Bible. As with most important issues, there are some pretty extreme views within some sections of the church. On one extreme there are people who believe homosexuals should be stoned (with stones, not drugs!). At the opposite end of the scale are people who think we should be ordaining homosexuals as priests or ministers. Neither group have really tapped into what the Bible says in full.

There are four major sections of the Bible which deal directly with the subject of homosexuality:

i) The story of Sodom and Gomorrah (Genesis 19:1–13);

ii) Leviticus, the Israelite people's instruction book on how to please God—and live a long life! (Leviticus 18:22 and 20:13);

iii) Paul's description of a decaying society (Romans 1:22–32);

iv) Paul's lists of sinners who can never come into heaven's kingdom (1 Corinthians 6:9–19, 1 Timothy 1:8–11).

In downtown Sodom, the sin which offended God and made Him angry was sexual perversion. (The term 'sodomy', describing the act of anal intercourse, was taken from these people.)

Here's the scenario: when God's angelic messengers arrive in human form in Sodom, Lot invites them to stay overnight at his house. Actually, he insists that they do, probably because he knows how unsavoury things can be out on the streets.

That evening the men of Sodom roll up at the door and insist that Lot brings his visitors out so they can have sex with them. (These visitors were probably good-looking—can you imagine an *ugly* angel?!)

In the Eastern culture of Bible times, allowing harm to come to a visitor to your house was considered the ultimate shame. So Lot does a thing which is horrifying in itself. He says, 'Hey, leave these guys alone, they're honoured visitors. I'll send my daughters out to you instead and you can have your way with them!'

(*Note:* Not every behaviour described in the Bible is pleasing to God!) The men of Sodom are not satisfied with that and try to attack Lot himself.

Thankfully the angels work a miracle which shuts the

whole explosive episode down. But what a mess of a place! In the end the town is wiped out because of the perversion of its people. Part of that perversion was a homosexual lifestyle.

In Leviticus, the people of Israel are told by God not to allow a man to 'lie with' another man in the way a man and woman would lie together. This, the passage says, is 'detestable' to God. The verse on homosexuality is stuck between two others: one warns against sacrificing children to the fiery god 'Molech'—a common practice among some ancient cultures—the other forbids having sex with animals. Any of these practices, it says, would cause the nation to be 'defiled' in God's eyes. God would be forced to turn His eyes away from a nation because of any of these. In Leviticus, God says He is as offended by homosexuality as He is by seeing children thrown into the fires of Molech!

In the New Testament things don't get any brighter for homosexuality (though homosexuals *are* given great hope for change through Jesus!). The great Christian pioneer Paul says that one of the signs of the destruction of a society is the fall of people into acts like those involved with homosexuality. He talks in Romans 1 about men who 'abandoned natural relations with women and were inflamed with lust for one another'. Men, he says, 'committed indecent acts with other men'. Paul says this shows a 'depraved mind'. He claims that when people do things like this, abandoning God's way of doing things, they may think they're wise but they have become 'fools' (Romans 1:21–24).

In his first letter to the Christians at Corinth, a real hot-spot for sexual slackness, Paul lists the homosexual lifestyle as one of the ways which will cut people out of God's kingdom. The list also includes idolaters, adulterers and male prostitutes, as well as thieves, swindlers and drunkards. He adds that while some of the Corinthian Christians were into all these things, they were now clean and set apart for God's use because they were followers of Christ. They weren't left to rot in their old way of life—*even homosexuals can be free through Jesus!*

Then, in one of his very last letters, Paul tells his protégé Timothy that practising homosexuals, like adulterers and murderers, are breakers of God's law and rebels against His plan.[21] What they do, he says, is the opposite of all good Christian teaching.

What does Jesus say about homosexuality? Nothing, directly. But then He didn't mention incest, rape or bestiality either. He probably didn't need to spend too much time on these because they were already 'no-no's' in His day. But over and over again Jesus upholds the Old Testament code which included teaching against homosexuality.

Jesus had compassion on people who had fallen morally but He never excused what they did. He forgave them—but only if they were prepared to leave the 'old life' behind (See John 8:3–11.)

Just one more thing needs to be said here. The Bible actually *encourages* people to have close and meaningful friendships with people of the same sex. David and Jonathan were great buddies, Ruth and Naomi were as close as two women could be, and Jesus had a very close friendship with John His disciple. (See: 1 Samuel 18:3–4; 20; John 13:27–36; 21:7,20; Ruth 1:16–17.) But none of these relationships had any sexual aspect.

Our problem in the late twentieth century is that desire to make sex the highest common denominator in all relationships! We've almost made sex seem an indispensable part of life! But the greatest relationship possible for a human being is not sexual at all—it's a spiritual relationship between us and our Maker.

Is AIDS the judgement of God on homosexuals?

Fair question—and one for which there's a short answer: *yes and no!*

Yes, God does judge sin. His holy, pure nature must deal with things which are impure and unholy. I don't know about you, but I find it kind of comforting to think that a pure God rules the universe. I mean, what hope would there be for us if the Big Guy with His finger on the button really was a bit shady in character?!

We can see something of God's judgement of wrong all around us if we look. In creation itself you can see how weeds grow and earthquakes shatter whole cities. Those are, in a general sense, the judgement of God who is allowing us to reap what we've sown in disobeying Him. In a *general* sense, AIDS is the judgement of God—it's part of what we reap for mistreating His gift of sex.

In a *specific* sense, though, AIDS is not God's judgement against homosexuals. Firstly because it's not only the homosexual community which is affected by this killer disease. Although the homosexual community is still experiencing the spread of AIDS more than any other part of society, many heterosexual people and drug-abusers have also contracted HIV, the virus which leads to AIDS. So have many innocent people, including unborn babies whose mothers are HIV positive.

Secondly, God does not specifically judge sin in this way—not in this life anyway. Think about it—if He did knock people down every time they did things which offend Him, we'd be stepping over dead bodies in the streets! And nowhere does the Bible suggest that homosexuality is any worse a sin than most others. Sure, there will come a time when we'll each answer to God for how we've lived, but we haven't arrived at that day yet. *Which is great news—because there's still time to get things right.*

(For more discussion on AIDS and how it works, see my book *Youth: The Endangered Species,* Word Books, 1993).

Are homosexuals ever cured?

Actually 'cure' is not a good word for what we mean. 'Recovery' is better. Remember Sy Rogers, former gay man and would-be-woman? What happened at the end of his story? . . .

> Realising that I hadn't managed my life very well on my own, I finally began sincerely seeking God. It was my re-ignited faith in God that led me down a path I once thought impossible for me. It wasn't that I stopped being gay. I didn't know 'how'—or if it was possible. I was, however, willing to stop living my life on my terms. Instead, I yielded to God on His terms . . .
>
> Today I very much enjoy the opportunity to live beyond my past problems. I enjoy being a husband and . . . a father. It isn't proof that I'm not gay, but it is evidence of a life I never thought possible.
>
> My recovery process took time and work and the

encouragement and accountability of (*sic*) my support-
ive friends. More importantly, my recovery depended
on my willingness to cooperate with God.

'Over the years and around the globe, everyone
that I personally know—or know of—that has overcome homosexuality has been enabled to do so as a
direct consequence of a life yielded to God and committed to the way of Christ . . . I am able to live beyond
being a homosexual.'[22]

According to Rogers and other experts in counselling
homosexuals, the key ingredients for recovery are: a desire
to change, a willingness to ask for help, a determination to
grow beyond the problem no matter what, and a great support group who believe it will happen. *Support is so important.*
After all, if the most common forms of homosexuality are born out of rejection (especially by same-sex
parents), then further rejection only drives sufferers away
from release.

A Christian friend shared with me how he had been
secretly wrestling with same-sex attractions for years. He
had never indulged in homosexual behaviour and he'd
almost resigned himself to a life without sexual activity of
any kind. As a boy and young teenager, his father had
never affirmed him in any direct way, had never touched
him positively or noticed him when he did well.

Through a series of events, he came to share his
anxiety with me and with a couple of trusted Christian
counsellors. Just being able to talk about it, he said,
without having anyone turn their heads in shame, brought
him release. He was able to get on with life and come to a
gradual but real recovery.

OK, so how does recovery happen? The first step in

recovery is knowing that homosexual practice is not pleasing to God (who loves us), it is unnatural (He made us for something more suited to us) and it is harmful to us (He wants to make us whole). Some help programmes which reach out to hurting homosexuals are opposed by gay lobbies because those lobbies won't admit there's anything wrong with the 'gay' way. Lobbies often become the main hindrance to the growth of those who want help.

And growth is the right word—that's what this recovery is all about. Rogers says, 'Quite literally those in recovery "grow beyond" their same sex fixation and "grow out of" their homosexuality. This growth, however, is a lengthy process—lengthier for some than others.' For many, he says, ' "recovery" can be a lifetime commitment.'[23]

So we're talking about a journey out of emotional immaturity. A process of getting over the psychological hurdles which have stopped people from living as God created them to live. Recovery may not mean the person marries—some people may never feel a great sexual attraction to the opposite sex. (A great many do.) But they *can* come to a point of forming same-sex relationships which are not erotic, and go on to lead lives which are blessed by God and free from guilt or shame.

Getting through to healing can take time and some times people fail along the way, even with the best of counsellors. But if there are good supporters around to encourage and understand (and hold the person accountable for their progress) there can be healing and liberty.

REFERENCES:

1.& 2. Francis Schaeffer, *The Letters of Francis Schaeffer*, ed. by Lane T. Dennis, p.194. (The editor notes that in later years, Schaeffer himself placed less and less emphasis on homophilia and more on 'the sinfulness of all homosexual practice'.)
  3. *Guide* magazine, October 1987, quoted by McIlhenny and York, *When the Wicked Seize the City* (Huntington House Pub., 1993), pp.19–20.
  4. Quoted by George Grant, *The Family Under Seige* (Bethany House Pub., 1994), p.173.
  5. Sinclair Rogers, *Questions I'm Asked Most About Homosexuality*, (Church of Our Saviour, 1993), p.20.
  6. Grant, op. cit., p.157.
  7. McIlhenny, op. cit.
  8. From 'The Advocate', quoted by Grant, op. cit., p.157.
  9. Rogers, op. cit., pp.25–26.
 10. Ibid., p.6.
 11. Ibid., p.6.
 12. Ibid., p.8.
 13. John Stott, *Issues Facing Christians Today* (Marshall Pickering, 1984), p.336.
 14. Reisman, Eichel, Court, Muir, *Kinsey, Sex and Fraud: The Indoctrination of a People* (Huntington House Pub., 1990), p.2.
 15. 'Now for the Truth About Americans and Sex', *Time* (17 October 1994), p.54.
 16. Reisman et. al., op. cit., p.17 and pp.57–58.
 17. Ibid., p.3.
 18. Ibid., p.4.
 19. Ibid., p.129.
 20. Grant, op. cit., p.166.
 21. In 1 Timothy 1:10 the word often translated 'pervert' is actually a Greek word which literally means 'male in a bed'. It indicates an 'active homosexual'.
 22. Rogers, op. cit., p.26 (emphases are his).
 23. Ibid., p.21.

Study Guide

Experts agree that love does not make the world go round, but it does make the ride a little easier to take.

Professor Claudius Fritzenbacher III
Emeritus Professor,
Dept. of Verifiable Myths, Camford University.

Warm-ups
What are some of the harmful attitudes people have towards practising homosexuals? Why are these harmful?

Study/Discussion
Look back over the story of Sy Rogers in this chapter. What do you think it suggests about how homosexual inclinations might begin in people? What do we mean by the term 'same-sex fixation' and how does this develop in a child or young teenager?

Read 1 Samuel 18:3–4; John 13:27–36. What do you think these passages tell us about same-sex relationships?

Read Romans 1:22–32; 1 Corinthians 6:9–19. What do you think these tell us about God's attitude to homosexual behaviour?

Read John 8:3–11. What is God's plan for people who are involved in any kind of immoral lifestyle?

Getting Started
A friend shares with you that they think they are gay. What can you do to help them, how can you advise them, without condoning homosexual behaviour?

Do some research for yourself on how AIDS is contracted and how it develops in the body.

Further Resources
Mal Fletcher, *Youth: The Endangered Species* (Word Books, 1993), chapter 4 (on AIDS, etc.).

8

IS HEAVEN GREEN?

– IS GOD A 'GREENIE'? –

*'Hey, I enjoyed your talk today—very interesting,' said
the young university student. 'But take a look at these
pictures. Don't you think Jesus would have cared about
creatures like these too? We've just got to do something
for them! Don't you agree?'*

I LOVE DOING UNIVERSITY missions. I like the people
and I love the buzz of speaking to men and women
who don't know a lot about Christianity. And I'm
fascinated by the many causes people take up in these
places. I learn something just about every time I set foot on
a campus.

This particular guy took me aside and showed me
photos of animals in the most horrific situations. There
were cats with their heads gripped in metal clamps. There
were rabbits with limbs bent and broken on science laboratory tables. These, I was told, were the innocent bit-part
players in the worldwide cosmetic industry. They were
having lotions applied to their skins and eyes to see
whether chemicals could be introduced into make-up
products for women. I have since read that clinical tests

support the idea that animals feel pain in much the same way humans do—even worms secrete certain chemicals to lessen their suffering.

I was forced to ask the question, 'What is God's attitude to animal testing?' And not just to this issue, but to conservation generally. Is God a card-carrying conservationist? *Is God green?*

Anyone for sci-fi?

You're strolling through your favourite part of town, taking in the sights, going about your normal business. Every once in a while you begin to wheeze and breathing becomes difficult. So you stop by a roadside vending machine, slip in a coin, put the supplied mask over your face and take a few whiffs of the oxygen you've just paid for. 'No, it couldn't happen,' you say. It is happening—in parts of Tokyo, *right now!*

When poisonous gases escaped from a chemical factory at Bhopal, India in 1984, 2,000 people were killed and 200,000 went blind! Even in less polluted places, many children need respiratory equipment just to help them through the day. Asthma and other breathing-related disorders are on the increase as pollens and pollutants mix as poisonous mid-air cocktails. We used to say something was as 'free as the air you breathe'—we might not be able to say that for too much longer. (One day we might all be living in Athens!)

Water is a cause for concern too. Have you ever been to the beach, itching for a swim, only to be confronted by a sign which said, 'Beach Closed: Health Alert'? Industrial pollutants can show up in water thousands of miles from the site where they were originally 'dumped', killing wildlife—and leaving you itching *after* your swim. When the *Exxon Valdez* ran aground, ten million gallons of crude oil devastated Alaskan wildlife. (Did you see the pictures of dead oil-soaked birds being pulled out of the black sludge?) More recently, in October 1994, 70 square kilometres of land and water in northern Russia were covered with sludge when *800 million litres* (that's two million barrels) of crude oil spilled from a ruptured pipe.

We're like farmers burning off our own crops—instead of skilfully farming the oceans we turn them into wastelands. In other places we overfish our seas, ruining the ecosystem which helps support us.

Chemicals are destroying our soil while CFCs and the like are trapping solar heat, preventing its escape and leaving us with the famous (or infamous) 'greenhouse effect'. Some people have predicted that this planetary overheating will cause polar ice-caps to melt, low-lying countries to flood and multitudes of people forced to leave their homes and move to cooler climates. Doesn't it it all sound a bit like a sci-fi movie from the fifties? Some predict you might live to star in it!

Entire rain forests in the Amazon are being razed to the ground, leaving many people in central Africa facing catastrophic droughts. The rain clouds which would once have brought them relief don't have anywhere to form (they're not called 'rain' forests for nothing!). We are using up natural resources, such as fossil fuels, as if they will last forever and we still haven't worked out quite what to do with nuclear energy. Many Europeans lived for a time under a radioactive cloud, courtesy of the Chernobyl nuclear power plant. Cancers, birth defects in babies and soil degradation in places have all been traced back to this disaster.

Alvin Toffler has said that we treat the world as though it were our 'petrol pump, garden, mine, quarry and cheap labour supply'.[1] We could add 'rubbish dump' to that list. When the plague ('Black Death') reared its head in India recently observers were blaming the rare outbreak on the government's 'enduring neglect of public hygiene'. They described cities as 'parables of urban squalor—filthy with refuse, aswarm with vermin and ripe with pestilence on a grand scale'.[2] Even in highly developed countries like the USA and Australia we're seeing the emergence of bacteria which are too powerful for existing drugs—and that hasn't happened for over sixty years!

Hey, I know I'm not telling you anything you haven't already seen in magazines or on the TV. The point is we need to get tired of reading about it—we need to get stirred up, to do something. But why bother—I mean, what's the point if God doesn't give a hoot? Maybe He knows something we don't know. Perhaps we're doomed anyway . . .

How did we get into this mess?

When I was in high school (and it was *not* Jurassic High!) the word 'environment' was only just coming into vogue. Nobody but 'eggheads' and eccentrics had used the word much before then—not in the way we use it now. Sadly, the whole trend towards widespread environmental concern is only a fairly recent development. 'Environment' is an industry in its own right now—with its own magazines, political lobbies and researchers.

So where does the problem begin? Here are a few of the factors which have led us to where we are environmentally:

1. Population growth

OK, let's start with the most obvious causes. In AD 1800 there were one billion (1,000 million) people sharing Planet Earth. As we've already seen the number exceeds five billion today. There are more people on our little planet today than have ever lived prior to this century. The big question on everyone's lips is, 'If one fifth of the world is dying of hunger today, how will we ever cope with the need in a few years from now?'

2. 'Progress'

Life magazine published a photo-spread called 'Saving the Endangered 100'.[3] It showed the top 100 most endangered species in America today and listed the threats against the survival of each one. The dangers ranged from 'prairie dogs' to 'power lines'. But over and over again words like 'illegal shooting', 'residential expansion' and 'off-road vehicles' came up. What's another word for all this? Progress.

Some people blame religions like Christianity for promoting a 'use and abuse' approach to the natural world. The real problem, though, has been caused by science! I mean, the Judaeo-Christian way of seeing the world existed for centuries before the scientific view came into vogue. Science and 'progress' as we now know them are fairly recent developments. So is ecological disaster. It was Descartes, not Jesus, who taught that the universe is more like a huge machine than a living organism. It was modern science which followed that line of thinking by teaching that we live in a 'closed system', that the material world is the only real one, that spiritual beings (including God) are not real. The human race lost something when it stopped believing it would answer to God for how it treats His Creation!

3. Self-hatred

If little green men visit our planet sometime next century, they might see our appalling treatment of the environment as a reflection of a poor self-image. Have you ever struck up a conversation with the town toughs who ride around in their cars with the windows down and radios turned 'up'? You know, the guys who throw cigarette packets from their windows, wolf-whistle at girls and kick cats down stairs. Many of these guys treat their environment and other people badly because they have a low opinion of themselves. There are many individuals—even whole cultures—who don't feel really great about who they are. They're often the ones most likely to take out their frustrations on the environment.

4. Abandonment

There are many people who have just given up on their environment. They've heard one too many TV reports on the state of things and it all just seems too big a problem to solve. Fatalism sets in, 'Well, maybe our children will do a better job . . . '

These days our commitment levels are generally well down on what they used to be. We tend to be turned-on to an issue for a while because it is the topic of conversation at the office, only to move on to other things when the fascination wears off. (I'm speaking very generally here of course. But I don't think I'm far wrong.)

Power to the people!

This is the big one, the major reason for the current environmental crises—the quest for power. Francis Bacon said, 'Knowledge is power'. Mao Tse Tung claimed, 'Power grows from the barrel of a gun.' (A real fun guy, was Mao!) Marx taught that it's the control of money—or capital—which brings real power. All three schools of thought have their adherents today. I think there are two major areas in which the thirst for power is leading to the destruction of our environment.

The first involves the drive to control money, or material things. We all know that over the years many governments and businesses have shown little regard for the environment. They've been too busy getting rich quick to care about what damage has been done along the way. They've cut corners when it comes to safety procedures and ignored warnings when systems have been overloaded. They've treated people and resources as if they have some kind of 'divine right' to use what they want and throw what's left away.

But who is 'they'? Don't we, as one observer put it, 'get the governments we deserve'? Don't our governments and the companies we support tend to reflect our own values, aspirations and feelings? Greed is not something which begins at corporate level—greed, like charity, begins at home.

When my grandfather was a young 'buck', a man would buy his first car only after years of hard work saving for it. When he finally drove it home, it became a source of pride and he said to himself, 'I'm going to drive this till the day I die!' (He would even wear driving gloves—was it to keep the wheel clean?) Usually the car died before he did and when he finally took it to the breakers he'd be feeling, as they say in Westerns, 'mighty low'. Years later his grand-children would have to sit through hour after hour of stories about that great old car.

We don't tend to make commitments like that any more—not to things, and very often not even to people. We're in too much of a hurry to buy, use and throw away. When you feel no attachment to things around you, you start living as if the only thing that matters in the world is your gratification—and sell yourself short in the process. 'People lose something of their humanity,' says Tony Campolo, 'when they destroy life [in animals] in order to provide items of luxury for the affluent.'[4]

Manipulating microchips

The drive to control money is only one part of the power problem. There's also the desire to control technology. The greatest commodity today is not money, it's change. It seems that the only constant in the world is change. Even money is subject to change these days; we're using more 'plastic cards' every year. There's just no way things are going to stop changing—rapid, constant, brain-teasing, heart-stressing change is here to stay. In the seventies Alvin Toffler was warning us about the 'roaring current of change' and the 'disease of change' which, he said, would leave many people feeling increasingly disorientated. Change is a 'growth industry'.

Power usually comes to rest in the hands of those governments, companies and individuals who have adapted best to change, and who are in the position to regulate or even control the changes which occur in the lives of others. How is that done? By controlling the means through which most change comes—technology.

Technology is what drives most of the really important changes we're seeing around us. When the ethics professors sit down to talk about the pros and cons of in-vitro fertilisation, what are they dealing with? Technology. When womens' groups—rightly—bemoan the effects of virtual reality pornography, what are they talking about? Technology. So to control change, and stamp a certain direction on society, leaders want to dominate the development of new technologies.

Of course, technology is not bad in itself, it's amoral. It is you and I, the consumers, who decide whether it will be used for good or evil. Not all scientists are lunatics let loose in laboratories and not all politicians are moral 'airheads'. But it is true to say that in the race to get new technologies faster than the rest of the pack, scientists, government figures and business leaders don't always stop to ask the main questions. Questions like, 'Is what we're doing moral?' or 'Is what we're doing taking society somewhere good?'

Scientist Ralph Lapp has put it like this:

No one—not even the most brilliant scientist alive today—really knows where science is taking us. We are aboard a train which is gathering speed, racing down a track on which there are an unknown number of switches leading to unknown destinations. No single scientist is in the engine cab and there may be demons at the switch with most of society in the coaches looking backwards.'[5]

French author Jacques Ellul puts it this way: '[Today] everything has become "means". There is no longer an "end", we do not know where we are going . . . we set huge machines in motion in order to go nowhere.'[6] He adds a telling blow, 'I refuse to believe in the "progress" of humanity when I see from year to year the lowering of standards among men I know . . . when I see them cornered by circumstances and, as they suffer, becoming thieves and frauds, embittered, avaricious, selfish, unbelieving, full of . . . rancour.'[7] New technology—and more money—doesn't always lead to 'progress'.

In the race to control new money and new technologies it's not just the winners we should be wary of—many of the losers are dangerous to the environment too. When Saddam Hussein pulled his men out of Kuwait he left the skies burning as if to say, 'If I can't have it, I'll destroy it.'

Man = Cancer?!

Did you ever wonder why so many of the groups on the radical fringe of change in society seem to share people and resources? Why do the same people who chain themselves to trees also march in the streets for gay rights, then wave the radical feminist flag? What do these radical groups have in common?

Answer: *a driving ambition to turn society as we know it on its ear!* They want revolution. They're motivated by a spirit of rebellion against all of society's accepted, traditional values. That's their real agenda but you won't read about it in their glossy, government-funded brochures. Even within some respected environmental movements there are powerful lobbies which want to use the group's resources to change more than the natural environment.

Take Greenpeace, for example. Ask most people and they'll probably tell you Greenpeace is doing a good job as a watchdog trying to keep governments and big business honest. Greenpeace sees itself as a kind of green conscience for the entire world. They've had some great TV coverage thanks to their protest-pacifism methods, which are based on the Quaker idea of 'public witness'. The theory goes that you can focus attention on some undesirable action by simply being there when it's carried out. It's a method which has certainly drawn attention to some evil practices. Yet even Greenpeace resorts to peddling propaganda in its push for change.

Groups like this have always used hyperbole—deliberate and graphic exaggeration—to make a point. For example, Paul Watson, a Greenpeace officer, says, 'We, the human species, have become a viral epidemic to the Earth.'[8] A prominent financial supporter of Greenpeace and representative of the Rockefeller Foundation goes even further, 'The world has cancer and that cancer is man.'[9] These are exaggerations, yet they have no doubt influenced people like Dave Foreman. He is a former member of Greenpeace who now calls on terminally ill patients hoping to persuade them to become eco-terrorists, to commit suicide on an environmental issue by strapping explosives to themselves and blowing up bridges and dams. *You're a dangerous guy, Dave!*

Hyperbole is a legitimate way to make a point, *as long as* everyone can see the exaggeration. If you've hidden that, you're lying. Greenpeace regularly takes several largely unrelated problems and packages them under one umbrella as if they are all connected. In this way they build up a picture of total ecological disaster and manipulate people's emotions and purse-strings in the process. One of the founders of Greenpeace, Patrick Moore, has now said that 'Greenpeace has moved from spreading disinformation to spreading hate.'[10] There are hidden agendas here.

Here's the point: setting the environmental agenda shouldn't be left in the hands of the 'expert' groups who dominate media stories. We can't place our trust in these groups simply because they make all the right noises and paint rainbows on their flags. And we can't improve things by simply throwing money at their programmes. The responsible course of action is for each of us to become better informed about the real issues—not the hype—and to do what we can to make things better.

Where's the church?

Nobody will tell you this on the six o'clock news, but one of the largest and fastest growing groups of people in the world today is the Christian church. Hundreds of millions of people drawn from every nation and culture call themselves active believers in Christ.

What's more, *the church is growing*, and not just because of population increase. There are now ten million charismatic Christians in the world. Their numbers tripled in the seventies and eighties—and they represent just one section of the worldwide church! So where have all these people been while the environmental debate has raged on?

It seems the church has been pushed to the fringes of the debate on ecological issues. (And the New Agers have moved in to fill the vacuum, offering to bring a certain spirituality to the whole deal.) Part of the reason for this would have to be the great differences of opinion within the church worldwide. Some Christians and church groups are passionately committed to saving the planet, others would rather save souls than save whales. Some are fatalistic about it all, 'Oh, well, we know things are going to get worse before the end. Why bother about it?' Others even see the threat to our natural habitat as a positive thing, 'It's a sign that Jesus is about to return, so it can't be all bad!'

Another reason that the church does not *appear* to be doing much, is the anti-church bias shown by media groups in some parts of the world. These groups come at the church with this attitude: 'You're a Christian? . . . And you want to get on TV? . . . OK, so go and do something incredibly stupid, dangerous or immoral!' You just don't get to hear about the good goals being scored by the Christian team. So what *does* the Bible have to say about the environment, if anything? What hope can it give us? Should Christians be involved with 'green' concerns?

You're not a monkey who got lucky!

Even Charles Darwin had problems believing the human eye could have evolved by natural selection! 'To suppose that the eye,' he said, 'with all its inimitable contrivances for adjusting the focus to different distances, [and] for admitting different amounts of light . . . could have been formed by natural selection, seems, I freely confess, absurd in the highest degree.'[11] Yet Charlie believed it anyway!

In fact the eye is one of the great evidences for

creation. In recent years, it's been discovered that the eye makes three tiny and almost unnoticeable movements. They're caused by minute contractions in the six muscles on the outside of each of our eyes. It's only because they automatically shift the position of your eyeball every fraction of a second that you can see anything at all. These muscles wobble your eye thirty to seventy times per second! (That's a lot of wobbling in a lifetime.) One of these three forms of eye movement, called a tremor, causes the cornea and the retina (front and back) of your eyes to move in circles with diameters of only 1/10,000 of a millimetre. That's about seventy times smaller than the thickness of this piece of paper.[12] Unbelievable, you say. Yes, it is unbelievable, if you *don't* accept that you're the work of a fantastic designer!

We are not monkeys who got lucky! And that's important in the context of environmentalism, for three reasons:

1. Love makes the world go round

Catholic thinker Pierre Teilhard de Chardin taught us that because God is at the centre of all things it is love which holds the universe together. Evolution has *competition* at the core of all things. Darwin's theory is based on organisms and species competing for their place in the survival stakes. Creation, however, puts *cooperation* at the hub of the universe. God is a Triune being in whom Father, Son and Holy Spirit all work together as equal and complementary expressions of divinity. God's creation simply reflects that spirit of cooperation which is part of His nature (Genesis 1:26). This should encourage us to work with creation, not against it.

When God gave humankind 'dominion' over the earth (Genesis 1:28, KJV), He did not mean 'domination'! He does expect us to make use of creation, but not *to use it up* then throw it away. To do so is not only ecological suicide, it's sin!

2. We are accountable to God (not just Greenpeace!):

The creation teaching of the Bible holds us accountable for the way we treat nature, not just to each other or to the creation itself but to the Creator. The natural universe was not made primarily for our consumption, or even our enjoyment, but for the glory of God. Nobody expresses that better than the great song-writers of the Bible, the psalmists. The writer of Psalm 8, for example, looks wide-eyed across creation and says:

> When I consider your heavens,
>   the work of your fingers,
> the moon and the stars,
>   which you have set in place,
> what is man that you are mindful of him,
>   the son of man that you care for him?
> You made him a little lower than the heavenly beings
>   and crowned him with glory and honour.
>
> You made him ruler over the works of your hands;
>   you put everything under his feet:
> all flocks and herds,
>   and the beasts of the field,
> the birds of the air,
>   and the fish of the sea,
>   all that swim the paths of the seas.
>
> O LORD, our Lord,
>   how majestic is your name in all the earth!

This guy ain't singing the blues! The writer of these lyrics is surrounded by the glory of God and it takes his breath away. But notice too, part of what makes him stand in awe is the special way human beings are blessed in creation. Human beings are not simply another species in nature. They are unique among all God's creatures, made a 'little lower than the heavenly beings', made to reflect something of the image of God which animals were not given. In Genesis it was only humankind who received God's 'breath of life' (Genesis 2:7). God made us spiritual beings with the ability to think rationally and philosophically and to thirst after fellowship with Him.

When modern environmentalists place man on a par with dolphins—wonderful as dolphins are—they're not just demeaning human beings, they're insulting God. They fit Paul's description of people whose 'thinking became futile . . . [and who] worshipped and served created things rather than the Creator' (Romans 1:22,25). Knowing that we are given special rights and responsibilities before God can be a powerful stimulant to treating creation the right way!

3. God gets involved in His creation

Christianity doesn't teach that God is a part of the natural world, as pantheistic religions do. If I build a chair I am expressing something of me in that chair—but the chair is not me, I still exist separately from what I've made. That's the way it is with God. Yet, because the Earth is His creation, He won't just stand by and watch it being torn apart.

Throughout the Old Testament we find God giving many instructions about proper treatment of the environment. Israel is told, in no uncertain terms, that it's to take good care of what essentially belongs to God.

In the Jewish law books, for example, God commanded that His people bring one tenth of their annual produce to the nation's priests, as a symbol that all they owned was God's (Leviticus 27:30). And any sale of land was not to be seen as a permanent thing, because it was God's possession—He could give to whomever He wanted (Leviticus 25:23). The people were constantly aware that they would give an account of how they treated their natural environment.

The Israelites were also under instruction to give the Earth a 'year of rest' every seventh year (Leviticus 25:5). They were not to sow the fields, prune vineyards or harvest crops in that year. This wouldn't be a bad policy today, given the problems we're facing with overfarming. Every seventh year even the vines had to be left to regenerate. God's concern was to see that 'the land will yield its fruit' (Leviticus 25:19).

According to Psalm 24:1, 'The earth is the LORD'S, and everything in it . . . ' God still hasn't finished with His creation!

If trees could scream . . .

Mr Klausner is a quiet, weird little man. He spends his evenings in his tiny garden shed playing around at his workbench. He's fascinated by the fact that in nature there are hundreds, perhaps thousands, of sounds human beings can't hear, because their frequencies are too high or too low for our ears to detect. Perhaps, he thinks, even plants can talk—we just can't hear them.

So he invents a little box which will help him hear the inaudible sounds of nature. One summer night he takes his black box filled with wires and dials into the front garden. He places the headphones over his ears and turns the dials. He hears a sudden shriek.

Looking around for the source of the painful sound he notices that his neighbour has just cut a rose from her bush. He asks her to cut another. She obliges, thinking him a strange little man anyway, and he hears the shriek again, just as the scissors slice through the stem.

Now he's *really* onto something! Very early the next morning, before dawn, he goes into the park across the road, armed with his little box and an axe. He puts on his headphones, lifts the axe, and swings deep into a huge, old tree. At the moment of impact he hears a low, mournful sound. It's so intense, so filled with sadness and pain, that he throws the axe aside and runs indoors to ring his doctor. When the startled physician arrives, little Mr Klausner orders him to put iodine on the cut in the tree, which he does—mainly because Klausner is looking menacing with that axe!

'*Another story from the Bermuda Triangle?*' you ask. No, just a tale from the imaginative mind of Roald Dahl.[13] But one that makes you think. If plants *could* talk, or sing, or cry, what would they tell us?

According to Romans 8, they would tell us they can't wait for Jesus to return. In Romans 8:19–22 Paul says that all creation is in 'bondage to decay' and 'groaning as in the pains of childbirth', waiting in 'eager expectation for the sons of God to be revealed.' The day will come, says Paul, when Jesus will return to claim those who have believed in Him. Then their mortal bodies will be changed to take on immortality (1 Corinthians 15:51–54). And not only will they be renewed, so will creation itself.

According to the Bible, nature right now is *not* the way it was first created to be—beautiful though it undeniably is. Because the first human beings were given oversight of God's garden, the decisions they made would affect all of creation. When Adam and Eve decided they'd had a 'better offer' than the one God gave them they were banished from the idyllic garden paradise which had been their only home.

But they weren't the only ones to suffer. The whole ecosystem went through a painful metamorphosis. The ground broke out in weeds and the soil became hard to till (Genesis 3:17–19). The first man and woman found that, no matter how hard they might try, they could never go back to the blissful way things were before. The stunning garden they had known as home was suddenly closed to all visitors (Genesis 3:24). Since that time, as Tony Campolo puts it, 'a mean and threatening spirit has become omnipresent in nature.'[14] But it won't always be this way!

'If I could talk to the animals,' sang Dr Doolittle. A very noble dream, Doc, but you weren't the first to try to converse with 'critters'. Francis of Assisi claimed that we could experience the grace of God in a special way through fellowship with the animals. In his part of the world people still love to tell stories about how he would tame wild beasts and how animals would run to him for his blessing. Now that may be a bit far-fetched, but Francis certainly felt something of the heart of his Lord.

You've heard of talking to the flowers, but what about speaking to the wind, or the waves? Jesus did it. During a storm He told them to 'be still' and—much to the amazement of His most ardent followers—they did (Mark 4:39–41)! He was commanding the natural world to respond to the 'shalom', the peace and balance, of God. He also elevated humble flowers to new heights when He pointed to lilies and claimed that even Solomon, the richest of all Israel's kings, had never been dressed as well as them (Mark 6:29). He said that birds could teach us a thing or two—they don't get uptight like humans do, because their Father in heaven takes care of them (Luke 12:24–25). At the very beginning of His public ministry Jesus was called 'the Lamb of God'; even humble sheep were dignified by His ministry (John 1:29).

Jesus, according to the Bible, is the style of things to come. Through Him creation is to be redeemed, or brought back from its bondage to decay. One day nature won't cry any more, wolves will lie down next to sheep and leopards alongside goats and little children shall play with them all as pets (Isaiah 11:6–9). Too incredible to believe? Most environmentalists would probably think so.

Environmentalists don't go far enough!

The problem with environmentalists is not that they aim too high, but that they don't aim high enough! Most responsible environmental groups today would settle for far less than God's great restoration programme. That's because they ignore two important facts.

Firstly, that man's behaviour isn't the only problem. Nature itself is no longer 'normal'. It is perverted, twisted away from God's original plan. Secondly, environmentalists completely ignore the issue which is at the very heart of the problem—man's moral rebellion against God. Why don't environmental groups talk about this? Because it's too close for comfort, that's why!

If I admit that a moral fall is what started the ball of destruction rolling, I face certain uncomfortable truths. Number one: if there are universal rules to keep, there must be a universal Rulemaker, a supreme God. Number two: if I admit there's a God and that He has a moral code for me to live by, then I have to confess that I haven't kept His standards. Number three: if I'm really honest I'll have to admit that I probably never will meet His high standards—none of my forebears ever did! That puts me in a spot. There's no way I can save either myself or my natural environment on my own. Woe is me.

But wait, this is where the Bible brings certainty and hope which even Greenpeace can't give! As we've already seen, the God of the Bible is a very hopeful person. The word 'hope' appears over fifty-eight times in the New Testament alone. God is not reaching for the headache pills when it comes to humanity's problem, and He is not stressing out thinking about what to do for the environment. He has already come up with a radical solution and He is working at it right now.

When Jesus died, He died to redeem *everything.* Yes, everything. Not just the human race, but nature as well. God is working to a plan which will see it restored to its original glory. In fact, He can even do better than that— He is going to build a 'new heaven and a new earth, the home of righteousness' (2 Peter 3:13). In this new world the moral problem will no longer be present, because immorality (and those who *wilfully* hold onto immoral living) will have been sent away, far away, to a place you wouldn't want to visit—not even in your worst nightmares.

Right now though, God is going right to the heart of the problem, the rebellious heart of mankind. His first concern is to get moral failure out of us, to make us spiritually right with Him. And that's possible only through faith in the death and resurrection of His Son, Jesus Christ.

When we admit our own total depravity—our inability to purify ourselves—and place our faith in Jesus alone to save us, we invite God's Spirit to start renewing us. We immediately become 'a new creation' spiritually (2 Corinthians 5:17). We become heirs of His promise to make us new physically too. Then there'll be no more crying for us, and no more pain in nature.

God has begun His environmental rescue operation, but He has had to start where the problem began—*with the human heart*.

Doing your bit now . . .

OK, so we know God's long-term agenda. Does that mean we should just sit back, Coke in hand and watch while the environment goes down the drain? Absolutely not! God will still hold us accountable for doing what we can. If you're a Christian, you won't be environmentally conscious simply because it's trendy. You'll be doing your best to preserve God's creation because it is God's, because His Spirit lives in you and you want to please God. Christians are not fatalists. They live to challenge the status quo, because they know there is something better to be had! So what can we do for the environment between now and the day Jesus returns?

1. Become a Christian!

Start the renewal process with *you*. Recognise that when Jesus died He did so to remove the stain of your sin before God. Admit that there's no other way for you to be saved than through what He did. Ask God's forgiveness for all your sins—not just the environmental ones. Accept His forgiveness. Now the 'new creation' process has begun in you.

2. Start rebelling

As a Christian you are called to change things around you, to influence your world for God's glory. Start thinking and asking questions for yourself—don't just accept what environmental groups sell you. (Watch for hidden agendas.) Stay informed on the issues, even when it's not so trendy.

3. Allow God to de-greed you

The less 'things' you buy and throw away, the less things there are to clutter up the environment. Don't buy on impulse. Plan before you buy. And stop praying, 'Lord, help my neighbours to stop buying things I can't afford.'

4. Buy 'Green'

Wherever you have the choice, deliberately support products which you know are environmentally friendly (recyclable, biodegradable, etc.).

5. Don't waste resources

Think lean and travel light. Make conscious decisions to limit your wastage of naturally generated fuels (electricity, gas, petrol, etc.). Try car-pooling to the office. The key is not necessarily 'austerity' but 'efficiency'.

6. Vote carefully and prayerfully

Take your civic responsibilities seriously. Become involved in community issues. If there's a green-care group operating on your campus or in your community, find out what their agenda is. At the very least get involved through the ballot box. Before you vote, ask questions like, 'What does this candidate do (not just say) to support better caring for God's creation?' Stay hopeful—hope is eternal if you're a Christian (1 Corinthians 13:13).

REFERENCES:

1. Quoted by Tom Sine, *Wild Hope* (Monarch, 1991), p.29.
2. James Walsh, 'Return of the Black Death', *Time (Australia)*, (10 October 1994).
3. *Life*, September 1994.
4. Tony Campolo, *How To Rescue The Earth Without Worshipping Nature* (Word Books, 1992), p.70.
5. Quoted by Alvin Toffler, *Future Shock* (Pan Books, 1971), p.390.
6. Jacques Ellul, *The Presence Of The Kingdom* (Helmers and Howard 1989), pp.51,53.
7. Ibid., p.99.
8. Quoted by George Grant, *The Family Under Seige* (Bethany House Pub., 1994), p.105.
9. Ibid., p.106.
10. Ibid., p.117.

11. Tom Wagner, 'Darwin vs. The Eye', *Creation ex Nihilo* magazine (Sept.–Nov. 1994).
12. Ibid.
13. From Roald Dahl, *More Tales Of The Unexpected* (Penguin Books, 1949).
14. Campolo, op. cit., pp.41–43.

STUDY GUIDE

Scientists now know that if human beings became extinct, this would represent a serious threat to life as we know it.

Professor Claudius Fritzenbacher III
Emeritus Professor,
Dept. of Verifiable Myths, Camford University.

Warm-ups

What current ecological issues concern you most? What are some of the causes of these particular problems?

Study/Discussion

I've quoted a scientist as saying, 'No one—not even the most brilliant scientist alive today—really knows where science is taking us. We are aboard a train which is gathering speed, racing down a track on which there are an unknown number of switches leading to unknown destinations . . . ' What is your response to this statement, and why?

Read Psalm 24:1; Genesis 3:17–19; Leviticus 25:5, 19–23; Romans 8:19–22. What do you think these passages have to say that will help us deal with ecological issues?

Read Genesis 1:28. What does it mean to 'subdue' the Earth? Can we do this in an 'environmentally friendly' way? How?

I've written about the wonders of the human eye as one evidence for creation. Can you think of some others?

Can you identify some products which you know have been developed using experimentation on animals? Can we stop this kind of experimentation altogether? Should we? Where do you draw the line on this issue?

Getting Started

What can you do this month to lift your game, ecologically speaking? What can your church/youth group/university club etc. do to become more involved in a balanced way?

Further Resources

Tony Campolo, *How to Rescue the Earth Without Worshipping Nature* (Word Books, 1992).

Tom Sine, *Wild Hope* (Monarch, 1991).

9

DID JESUS HAVE A STOCKBROKER?

– GOD'S CREED ON GREED AND NEED –

Hey, are things feeling a little crowded for you these days? Perhaps it's because there are 5 billion other people sharing this tiny planet with you—and that number's expected to balloon to 6.2 billion by the turn of the century. Twenty per cent of the people on this globe are destitute, lacking even the basic necessities of life. They have no clean, safe water supply. Meanwhile, back on the farm, another 20 per cent of us live on 80 per cent of the world's income.

AROUND THE GLOBE WE are seeing rapid population growth—especially in countries which could do without it—and with it a widening gap between the rich and the poor. Famine is on the increase and new outbreaks of old diseases, like plague, threaten to wipe out whole sections of populations.

At the same time, the rich industrialised countries seem to get richer. Smart machines are making life easier than ever, for those who have the cash (or plastic) to afford them. We've got 'smart' cars, with on-board computers to tell us how to get where we're going. There are 'smart' houses, where computers will regulate the temperature in each room according to each person's tastes. Soon we'll see the introduction of 'smart' cards—credit cards which have microchips to hold all your personal details, including your health records, library card number and so on.

So the poor get poorer and the rich buy new toys. What can be done to stop the rot?

Where to from here?

There's no easy solution to the world's economic woes and the injustices we see. Down through the millennia world movers and shakers have experimented with all kinds of economic systems as political fashions have come and gone.

At one time the trade in human slaves formed the foundation of many national economies. For centuries slavery was a huge multi-national industry. Stretching back to the earliest days of human history, it enjoyed a boom in the days of the Roman Empire. Everyone knows about the infamous American slave trade, the social effects of which are still being felt in urban America today.

More than fifteen million men, women and children were abducted from their homeland and sold to wealthy plantation owners in America during the 400 years of the slave trade. Another forty million Africans lost their lives during transportation.[1] But you won't hear much said about the two million Africans sold into slavery by the British in the West Indies; or the thousands of African slaves who were brought to South and Central America to work on the new sugar and coffee plantations owned by rich Europeans.

The feudal system had its day too. The general idea was that all land technically belonged to the ruling monarch who, in return for military service and taxes, would allow a gentry class of lords and ladies to hold land and administer justice. There were also a few middle-class merchants around, but the majority of the population were serfs, who served as cheap labour for the lord's land—and cannon fodder for the king's army. They were no better than slaves. This system generally declined from about the thirteenth century when a money economy started to take over, and with it trade, commerce and industry.

In more recent times we've had communism and capitalism fighting it out for their place in the sun. Both have made great promises about what they could do to make the world a better, fairer place.

Communism is a revolutionary brand of socialism which was first cooked up by the political philosophers Marx and Engels. They taught that the means of production in a society should be owned by the people. With the appearance of the Industrial Revolution's shining new machinery, a plethora of new products hit the market. Many of them were items of luxury or convenience— people didn't actually need them to survive. Karl Marx taught that rich 'capitalists' manipulated people's lives by teaching them to think they needed these things, and then by controlling the production of them.

Marx called for the overthrow of the rich capitalists. He advocated a 'dictatorship of the working classes' and believed that communism would eventually take over the world. Whether Karl and his friends foresaw it or not, their scheme became a brilliant political tool for dictators and tyrants. In most countries, their beloved workers became worse off under communism than they were before, and whole nations had the very soul ripped out of them. Today, communism has seen better times, but it's still a force to be reckoned with in many parts of the world.

Lined up against communism is its old foe capitalism. The capitalist way is based on the idea that the majority of production, distribution and exchange of goods in a society should be kept in private hands.

Producers, be they individuals or companies, will compete against one another for profit. In the meantime, governments will stay more or less out of the way and let the 'markets' control things—as in monetarism, championed by Milton Friedman—or actively inject more money into the system whenever the economy is doing badly—as with macroeconomics, the brainchild of John Keynes.

Today capitalism has the upper hand throughout most of the world. That's probably because it does *not* necessarily insist that there is no God—leaving the way open for people to pursue spiritual as well as material goals—and it *does* encourage individuals to develop their creative potential. Sadly though, its strengths have often been its weaknesses.

For a start, individual enterprise can easily become individual*ism*. Tony Campolo writes, 'Society under capitalism creates egoists who love things and use people, instead of persons who use things and love people.'[2] Also, healthy competition—which urges each player to improve—can sometimes turn into destructive paranoia, where nobody wants to share what they've gained with the next guy.

America is perhaps the most capitalistic country on

Earth, and it has some great things going for it. But over the last twenty years a new poorer class has emerged. If the seventies were the decade of 'Me', says American author Tom Sine, the eighties were the decade of 'Us and Them'.[3] In the USA today 23 per cent of the citizens are illiterate with violence breaking out in some communities as the have-nots become more and more resentful of the haves. In Chicago's South Side, each school term begins with a weapons search. Gangs are widespread. A school child and gang member was recently arrested by police who described him as a 'hardened criminal and killer'. He was fourteen years old![4]

Capitalism may be preferable to communism, but on its own it is not enough to guarantee a happy or equitable world.

Money makes the world go around?

If the best monetary system we've devised is not capable of bringing justice to the world, what hope is there? What can an emerging generation do to improve things?

We can make a start by at least identifying who the real enemy is. The basic problem in industrialised countries is not big business, or even mega-budget governments, it's materialism.

You mean the love of money? No, it's more than that. Materialism is a philosophy based on the idea that nothing exists over and above matter and the movement of matter. Everything there is can be experienced by the human senses, understood by the human mind and described in scientific terms. The universe is a closed system; there is no supernatural realm, and there is no God. And, the thinking goes, who needs Him anyway? I mean, we're getting better at this science thing all the time. We'll get the right answers to our problems if we play with the Rubik's cube for long enough.

Why do people always equate materialism with money? I suppose it's because you can tell whether a person is a materialist—whether they believe in a closed universe—by the way they handle money. If you don't believe in a God who holds us all accountable for how we live, you're more inclined to live a fairly self-centred life and your goals are more likely to be based on the acquisition of things.

This has been the problem for both communism and capitalism. 'Marxism,' claims George Grant, 'is the most materialistic of all social theories. It sees history through the lens of money.'[5] Hence the openness of this system to abuse by despots and dictators. If God's not there, who's to say I can't use other people to get what *I* want?

Capitalism, in the way most of us live it, also promotes materialism. We seek to do well not so much for the glory of God, or the improvement of others' lives, but for the material enrichment and comfort of our own.

There's nothing inherently wrong with money—it's just a tool. We can use it for good or for evil. But it's what we *do* with our money which shows the way we really think about the world. That's precisely what Jesus told us 2000 years ago, 'Where your treasure [money] is, there your heart [values] will be also' (Matthew 6:21). The problem is that most of us, being true materialists, place our faith in money and economic systems to solve our woes rather than trusting God. We like to think that money can bring certain benefits:

1. ***Power:*** We hope that money will help us to control circumstances, if not people, so that things go smoothly for us.

2. ***Certainty:*** We'd like to think that money can give us some sort of security in facing the future.

3. ***Individual expression:*** We think money can free us to find out and express who we really are.

4. ***Acceptance:*** We hope that money might help us gain the appreciation and respect of other people.

We can control money, but we can't control a Supreme Being. So the dollar might say, 'In God we trust', but in our hearts we know better!

God's attitude to material things . . .

So, is God against money or just apathetic about it? Neither, but there are many people who think that God has no interest in money (no pun intended), that He is only interested in intangible, spiritual things. That kind of thinking is based on three popular myths about God.

The first is that the human soul is important to God, but He is not too fussed about the body. The Bible claims that when God created human beings He made them complete, *not* independent bits and pieces which He decided to tack together at the last minute. The human body was *not* a divine afterthought: 'Gee, I guess I'd better wrap this spirit in a body of some kind!' In fact, those who place their faith in Christ are promised *new, resurrected bodies* when He returns. (Compare: Luke 24:39; 1 John 3:2 and 1 Corinthians 15:51–54.) Even in post-history eternity human beings will have bodies!

The second myth is that eternity is what counts with God, that He is not much interested in time. But the Bible talks about there being two sides to reality: time *and* eternity. They can't be compared with each other because they're so different. But we will be judged in eternity for what we did with our resources here in *time*.

What's the third myth? That God is more keen on sacred, religious things than He is on normal, everyday, secular things. In the Old Testament, however, God demanded only one day out of every seven be kept for us to rest and reflect on spiritual things. This was His day, the Sabbath. Most Christians now celebrate this on Sunday, of course, because this is the day when Christ rose from the dead. The other six days were for business as usual!

But doesn't the Bible warn against 'the flesh'? Yes it does, but that term actually refers to our lower, more base desires, not to physical cell tissue! No, the Bible paints a picture of a God who is very practical, even 'down-to-earth', when it comes to life in His real world.

God's attitude to poverty

God has absolutely *no problem* with money. In fact in the Bible some of God's best friends live on the wealthy side of the tracks! (Abraham, Job and Solomon for example.) He does, however, have a *massive* problem with poverty and the greed which often causes it.

John Stott says there are three basic groups of poor people listed in the Old Testament. The first is the 'indigent poor', those who are poor in the economic sense. They don't have enough of the bare necessities to survive. The second he calls the 'powerless poor'. These people are socially and politically oppressed. They're the ones Amnesty International is fighting for today.

In both of these cases, poverty destroys God-given human dignity. I've seen this first-hand, in countries like Sri Lanka where beggars in their forties sit on hot city streets with their legs twisted up beneath them. Many parents will break their childrens' limbs because they know it will help them later earn more money begging.

Finally, says Stott, there are the 'humble poor', those who acknowledge their reliance on God's help and place their hope in Him.[6]

God gave His prophets, priests and kings practical instructions for helping those in the first two categories. To help the economically poor, employers were to pay fair and prompt wages. Farmers were not to harvest their fields right up to the edges; they were to leave a little produce on the ground or on the vines for the poor to gather up (Leviticus 19:9–10). Every third year one tenth of their produce was to be given to the poor (Deutoronomy 26:12) and every seventh year fields were to be left fallow and vines unharvested. The needy could help themselves to whatever they could find still growing (Exodus 23:11).

To protect the powerless poor, God insisted that the courts were to be impartial—there was to be no bias on the basis of rank or wealth (Exodus 23:6; Psalm 72:1–4). Here's how Stott puts it, 'The biblical perspective is not the "survival of the fittest" but the "protection of the weakest".'[7] When you read the Old Testament it can seem that God is totally biased towards the poor. In actual fact He only seems that way because *we* are so far out of balance ourselves.

God *does* give some preferential treatment to the

poor—because they're so often sinned against and without an advocate. He also calls His people to stand up for the poor (Luke 14:12–14). But He *doesn't* love them any more because they are poor. In His moral judgement of human beings, He is not prejudiced by wealth *or* poverty—He does not have class enemies. That's the very thing the New Testament warns us against; making personal value judgements based on what a person has or doesn't have (James 2:1–4). God sets Himself against the rich who oppress the poor, *because they oppress the poor,* not because He is jealous of their wealth (Luke 1:46–53)!

The third group, the spiritually meek and dependent, were actually encouraged to hold onto their poverty! It's the attitude of a 'broken and contrite heart', which is most valuable to God (Psalm 51:17). God calls His people to *encourage* spiritual meekness and dependence on Him, but to do their best to *wipe out* material poverty.

Isn't eradicating all poverty just a little too much to hope for? Yes and no. For a start, even Jesus recognised that poverty will be an ongoing problem in this fallen world. He said the poor would always be with us (Matthew 26:11). But that wasn't a statement made in despair, because the Bible promises that poverty will be abolished when Jesus returns. Then God 'will wipe every tear from their eyes. There will be no more death or mourning or crying or pain, for the old order of things has passed away' (Revelation 21:4). Jesus was simply giving a realistic appraisal of the way things are in this age. For example, billions of dollars were poured into economic disasters like the Rwanda war but corruption in high places robbed the common people of much of the benefits. There's more to solving problems of poverty than throwing money at them.

Nevertheless, Christians are not called to live in complacency about this. They should behave with a mixture of *idealism* and *realism*. The realist in us sees how things really are and understands that the world's problems won't be solved until Jesus returns. Also the idealist in us wants to change things so it is more like God's kingdom now!

It is a tragedy that, according to some estimates, 62 per cent of global income is received by the church, and we spend 92 per cent of that on ourselves![8] The world around us has been given the right to decide whether we are really Jesus' disciples by the quality of our love, first of all to other believers and then to the world at large (John 13:35, 1 John 3:17).

So what does God want from me?

Traditionally, people have responded to world poverty by thinking in one of three ways. Some folks have opted for what's called in one book the 'Franciscan response'.[9] St Francis of Assisi was a fairly wealthy guy until he decided that God was calling to leave all that behind and devote himself to a life of poverty and service. People who like to follow his lead often do so with a simplistic view of world poverty. They feel that if they become poor, there'll be more for everyone else in the world. But how can the problem of poverty be solved by more poverty? How can you give to the poor out of empty pockets?

David wrote in one of his many songs that God blesses His people so that they can always be 'generous and lend freely' (Psalm 37:26). Francis may have been called to complete, *self-imposed* poverty, but that will not be God's call for every person. *(Did I hear a sigh of relief?)*

Even in the book of Acts, where people sometimes gave with great sacrifice to the work of the church, they still retained private property such as houses, land and so on. If they gave all away, it was not necessarily because God or the church had asked them to. (See Acts 2:44–47; 5:1–10.)

There are other people who face up to poverty with a form of prosperity theology which says, 'If you only have faith in God, you can get anything you want. If you're not wealthy, you're just not a person of faith!' Sounds nice, doesn't it? Until you read Bible scriptures which command us *not* to get hooked on wealth! Take, for example, Luke 12:15, 'Watch out! Be on your guard against all kinds of greed; a man's life does not consist in the abundance of his possessions.' Again, this view is far too simplistic about the causes of poverty.

I don't want you to think I'm coming down on the idea that faith in God works! God *has* promised to meet the needs of those who love and obey Him, and even to give them 'abundance' so they can generously bless others too. But more on that shortly . . .

Other people respond to the needs by making Christian doctrines out of either capitalism or communism. They defend either one as if they were what Jesus had in mind when He spoke about changing the world. As we've seen, both of these systems have been party to self-ishness and materialistic thinking—communists don't always share and capitalists are often too individualistic. Neither system is all it's cracked up to be—though I must admit I'd prefer to live in a capitalist society rather than a communist one.

It's not so much right *systems* the world needs but right *decisions*, right choices made on an individual and small group level. We *can* make a difference to the world's enormous economic woes, but the change must begin at home. Here are a few choices you can make now to make yours a more world-conscious, poverty-busting lifestyle:

1. Having faith

There's a phoney kind of austerity which says, 'If I have nothing, everyone else will have something.' Sadly, people who live by this rule are often more proud about their achievement—abject, snivelling poverty—than people who are wealthy. They seem to say to their world, 'I bet you wish you could be as righteous as me!'

Biblical faith is not like that at all. Faith doesn't focus on itself or its own achievements. A. W. Tozer wrote that faith is like an eye—the eye is real, but it's not aware of itself, it's too busy focusing on something other than itself. Faith, like the eye, must have an object and that object is God. 'Faith,' said Tozer, 'is the gaze of the soul on God.'

Faith in God means believing the promises He has made and changing your actions to *show* that you believe them—God isn't impressed by lip service! To fail to believe God's promises is to insult His integrity; it's as if you're saying, 'God doesn't keep His word, so I won't bother trusting Him.' The Bible is clear—God is, above all else, faithful and *good*!

However, real faith *doesn't* go out claiming things just because they're there. Sure, a little treat is OK now and again—God isn't stingy, though some religious people are! But 'serving' God just for what you can get out of Him isn't serving *Him* at all, and He knows what's in your heart. Real faith believes three things:

a) *Needs:* In Matthew 6:33 Jesus gave us one of the

207

greatest summaries of prosperity in the Bible, ' . . . seek first [God's] kingdom and his righteousness, and all these things will be given to you as well.' All *what* things? When you read the context, you find He is talking about necessities like food, clothing and shelter. But that *doesn't* mean He wants you and me to get by on a bare minimum, just clinging onto survival by our fingertips! In the same passage Jesus tells us that God is a good Father, who cares much more for us than for any other creature in His world, and will prove it in the way He looks after us (Matthew 6:25–30).

Jesus promised to give us life 'more abundantly' (John 10:10, KJV). 'Abundant' literally means 'more than enough', or 'overmuch'. In the King James Version of the Bible, the words 'abundance', 'abundantly' and 'abundant' appear forty-nine times. God is into giving us more than just enough! If you've placed your life in God's hands He will meet your needs, spiritually and temporally, and you'll usually have more than the bare essentials. But you must seek His kingdom first. His priorities and values must also be yours. *You must be living for something bigger than you are!*

b) ***Opportunities to share:*** Generosity is not a function of how much you have in the bank, it's an attitude. But more on that in a moment . . .

c) ***Opportunities to fulfil your destiny:*** Hebrews 13:20–21 says, 'I pray that the God of peace will give you every good thing you need so you can do what he wants' (NCV). Understand that *you* have a destiny to fulfil. God knows better than anyone what that destiny is, and what you will need to fulfil it.

In mid-1994, my family and I conducted a four-month mission to Europe, which included a five-week intensive assignment in Belfast, Northern Ireland. In that troubled city no ceasefire had yet been arranged and, along with a musician friend from Australia and my assistant, I was able to visit and encourage some pretty exciting churches (in some fairly dangerous places).

It was a great time and I thanked God for the opportunity to do it. But we wanted to do the whole thing without being a financial burden on the churches of Northern Ireland. So, months before we left we began praying for an extraordinary level of God's provision. We set a goal to raise $10,000 (Australian) for Northern Ireland alone. To my amazement, just a couple of weeks after we started praying someone gave it to us as a single donation! We hadn't even been on any great fundraising drive! After that we had to adjust our goals a little.

The point is, we were doing what we felt the Boss upstairs was leading us to do. We wanted to do something which God could bless. (Sometimes our endeavours are too small for God to 'fit into'!) The whole mission involved sacrifice on our part. We took our three small children and lived out of suitcases for sixteen weeks as we moved from event to event across Europe. *None* of the money we raised for Northern Ireland was used anywhere else but in that country, so we had to believe God would provide as we moved around. I presented around 150 public speeches in 120 days, and we endured a pretty hectic travel schedule. But God blessed our efforts, in more ways than one. We saw some remarkable things happen—and all of our financial needs were met, *with some to spare!*

I agree with Loren Cunningham, founder of Youth With A Mission, 'When God has spoken to you, go for it! God loves aggressive faith! Set your goals with a combination of individual initiative and God's leading . . . [and] never be half-hearted.'[10]

2. Living simply

So God doesn't want me to live in poverty. But He doesn't want to see the soul sucked out of me by a life of luxury and ease either! Luxury is *excessive* comfort which blunts the spiritual senses.

Again, material comfort isn't wrong in itself. Let's face it, it's much easier to concentrate on really giving your life to something big when you're not preoccupied with where your next meal is coming from! Martin Luther once believed that the only way to make God happy was to completely forego *all* of life's little comforts. In fact, he went one better—he used to whip himself until he bled, thinking that this proved his spirituality. (He wasn't a lot of fun at parties, old Martin!) That's what can happen to people who rely on their *lack* of comfort to prove their moral superiority.

Thank God, Martin's story didn't end there! The Reformation changed world history, for the better. And it all came about because Luther finally realised that having faith in God does not mean being a snivelling wretch all your days!

Nevertheless, *excessive* comfort, luxury, can bring on three dangerous traits. First of all it can encourage pride—we lose our poverty of spirit, our reliance on God. Jesus told the story of the bloated rich man who, totally deluded into believing that he deserved all he had—and forgetting where the blessing came from—decided to celebrate by building even bigger barns and partying until he dropped. 'You have plenty of good things laid up for many years,' he said to himself. 'Take life easy; eat, drink and be merry.' His refusal to acknowledge God in his life brought this rebuke, straight from heaven, 'You fool! This very night your life will be demanded from you. Then who will get what you have prepared for yourself?' (Luke 12:16–21).

Secondly, luxury can breed materialism—an unhealthy obsession with the things we own, to the point where they 'own' us. If we're serious about helping to change world poverty, we must start by adjusting to a lifestyle of *limits*. That means refusing to live by the old adage, 'If you've got it, flaunt it.' It means accepting self-imposed limitations on how we will use what we have. We will restrict our spending not because someone else demands that we do—that would be to live under a kind of Pharisaism—but because we have *chosen* to live for something bigger than we are, something that lives on when we die.

Luxury can also give birth to diabolical selfishness, which is based on a fear of losing all we have if we start sharing some of it around. Jesus told the tale of a 'rich man who was dressed in purple and fine linen and lived in luxury every day' (Luke 16:19–31). This guy was so in love with luxury itself that he completely ignored the beggar who sat at his gate, longing to eat even the crumbs which fell from his table. (This sounds a little like some countries today!) 'Even the dogs came and licked his sores', Jesus said. When both men died, it was Lazarus who was carried to heaven. The rich man, well, he went to another destination, and from there he could see Lazarus living in blessing. Remember, God has no problem with money, but He does have a problem with our ignoring the needs of others!

3. Being content
(Thanks for the good times . . .)

I love a good rags-to-riches story, but it's not often you read riches-to-rags stories. Even more rare are the *riches-to-rags-and-back-to-riches* type! The biblical story of Job is one such tale. Here's this guy who's got everything—the world is his oyster and he's got the world by the tail (which is kind of hard with an oyster!). Then he loses the lot, in a very short space of time, through no fault of his own. He hasn't done anything mischievous on his tax returns or embezzled company funds. Circumstances conspire against him and he's suddenly bankrupt and sick. All he has left is a handful of friends who turn out to be about as much comfort as a shotgun blast to the foot!

So what does he do? I know what I'd be doing—I'd be singing the blues with Eric Clapton, 'Nobody loves you when you're down and out!' But not Job. He turns his eyes heavenward and says, 'Naked I came from my mother's womb, and naked I shall depart. The LORD gave and the LORD has taken away; may the name of the LORD be praised' (Job 1:21). Is this guy certifiably insane? No, he's a man who *is* genuinely hurting, but he's also learned the lesson of contentment.

Contentment does *not* mean lying down and taking whatever life dishes up, without a whimper. In fact, as the story of Job unfolds you find him getting pretty feisty at times, and even a little aggressive with God! Real contentment is being thankful for what we *still* have, when our natural tendency in hard times is to focus on what we've lost.

Being content means seeing that every good thing you enjoy, no matter how small, is actually a gift from God.

When you get right down to it, He gives us the very air we breathe. If we're content our losses will still hurt. We may still cry 'foul!' *and* do everything we can in good faith to improve our lot. But we don't shake a fist at God and scream about how unjust He is. In the end, that turns out to be Job's only mistake (Job 31:35–37), but he repents of it and God honours him with more than he lost in the first place (Job 42:10)!

You could sum up the Bible's attitude to luxury with the wise words of Proverbs 30:8–9:

> Keep falsehood and lies far from me;
>> give me neither poverty nor riches,
>> but give me only my daily bread.
> Otherwise, I may have too much and disown you
>> and say, 'Who is the Lord?'
> Or I may become poor and steal,
>> and so dishonour the name of my God.

4. Giving dangerously!

There's a prevailing attitude in the world around us which says, 'The more I *hoard*, the more I'll *have*.' It's an attitude which stops a great many people from getting involved in alleviating the poverty around them.

It's a rationale which sometimes finds a place at the highest levels of international trade. Large countries fighting for an even larger slice of the economic pie—thinking that money alone brings security—while struggling smaller countries are left with the crumbs. They're eventually sent into bankruptcy because they can't repay the loans from world banks. Their people are destined to a future which holds nothing more than increasing interest payments, further indebtedness and greater powerlessness!

If you aspire to membership of the radical kingdom of God, you are called to take a very different view of things. Jesus, like the Old Testament prophets before Him, calls us to 'go the extra mile', to do better than 'pagans' do (Luke 6:27–36). It's no credit to us, He says, if we only lend to those from whom we can expect a return. And we shouldn't pat ourselves on the back if someone asks for our shirt and we give it to him. Big deal, says Jesus, even people who have no love for God do that! No, we should prophetically point the way beyond the status quo, to the way things *should* be—and *will* be one day, in the kingdom of God.

Jesus summed up for us His whole mission, His whole agenda for Planet Earth, with these words:

> The Spirit of the Lord is on me,
>> because he has anointed me
>> to preach good news to the poor.
> He has sent me to proclaim freedom for the prisoners
>> and recovery of sight for the blind,
> to release the oppressed,
>> to proclaim *the year of the Lord's favour*
> (Luke 4:18–19, italics added).

What's this 'year of the Lord's favour'? It's the Old Testament year of Jubilee. Once every fifty years there was supposed to be a time in Israel when all debts were cancelled; when if someone had lost their land through debt they could have it returned to them; and when all those in debtors' prison could be set free (Leviticus 25:10–55). I say 'supposed to be', because this law of God was never one the Jews actually kept. You see, it's never been *politically correct* to go the extra mile, to be generous. But it is *prophetically correct!*

Jubilee shows us what God's nature is like. He has been incredibly generous towards humankind—especially in the way He has forgiven our moral debts to Him—and He calls us to be just as generous with one another (Matthew 18:23–35). The spirit of Jubilee, which is the spirit of Jesus, is what God calls for—from governments, businesses and individuals.

But wouldn't the whole international money system collapse if we just let people out of their debts as easily as that?! Jesus did not teach that people shouldn't pay their debts. He warned that if we didn't repay a fair debt, and couldn't work things out with our creditor, we could expect the full weight of the law to come down on us (Luke 12:58–59).

No, what Jubilee is about is correcting the unfair advantage taken in so many debt situations—the use of power and privilege to put people in debt in the first place, for example. It's about giving the 'little guy' a real chance to climb out from under his mountain of debt! The kingdom of God is against the use of economic power to crush and hold lives to ransom. The spirit of Jubilee is the spirit of generously building hopeful people for a brighter future.

When you and I on an individual level give to organisations like Compassion or World Vision, we are helping people to get out of the hole poverty has dug for them. When we bundle up our old or unused clothes and send them off to the Salvation Army in the high street, we're providing a little breathing space for those who need time to put their lives back together. When we band together to form small groups who raise funds for the hungry or homeless, we are showing a little of the spirit of Jubilee. When we take that extraordinary offering in church to invest in the political refugees of Rwanda, we are doing what Jesus would do.

The key is to start thinking *globally*, and act *locally*. The important thing is actually crossing the street (or the world) to lift someone out of the dirt and get them started on the road to a better life. That's what it means to give dangerously, to go beyond the call of duty!

5. Building people . . .

So, (Sir) Bob Geldof didn't invent the idea of world-scale aid programmes—God did. He called the idea Jubilee, and Jesus came to share it with people of every nation. But there is one trap we can fall into when we give dangerously. We can so easily lay 'the guilt' on those to whom we give. 'Well, don't thank me,' we'll say. 'Really, it was nothing! . . . Then again . . . um . . . it *was* an effort. I mean, you *do* really owe me now. So, hey, *let me tell you how to run your life!*'

Error! Incorrect parameters! (As my computer would say.) Real Jubilee-mindedness is not about scoring points at other people's expense. It's about *releasing* people and helping them stand on their own feet, with God's help.

6. Avoiding the 'you'll do it my way' syndrome!

As far as the God of the Bible is concerned there are certain hard-and-fast-rules when it comes to money matters. We should avoid materialism and luxury which can lull us into a false sense of spiritual security. We must adopt a generous lifestyle.

But there are also some variables, some things which He leaves to our individual consciences—such as what kind of car we drive and what kind of clothes we buy. In these and other matters like them we should be guided by *general* Bible principles. In these areas the Bible makes no specific demands outside our moral responsibility to honour God and love others with what we have. We have no right to insist that everyone else must live as we do, drive the same sort of car, wear the same kinds of clothes and eat the same type of food.

In a nutshell, we should be prophetic, not Pharisaical. Yes, pray and sacrifice. Find a personal, biblical benchmark in money matters. Invest your life to the maximum in something which will outlive you! But *don't* make your rules into God's laws (Mark 7:6–7)!

REFERENCES:

1. *Hutchinson Softback Encyclopedia* (Random Century Group, 1991), p.761.
2. Anthony Campolo, *Partly Right* (Word Books, 1985), p.181.
3. Tom Sine, *Wild Hope* (Monarch, 1991), p.84.
4. *The World at Noon*, ABC TV (10 September, 1994)
5. George Grant, *The Family Under Seige* (Bethany House Pub., 1994), p.235.
6. John Stott, *Issues Facing Christians Today* (Marshall Pickering, 1984), pp.234–237.
7. Ibid., p.237.
8. Tom Sine, *Why Settle for More and Miss the Best?* (Word Books, 1989), p.168.
9. Sherman and Hendricks, *Your Work Matters to God* (NavPress, 1987), p.173.
10. Loren Cunningham, *Daring to Live on the Edge* (YWAM Pub., 1991), pp.142–143.

STUDY GUIDE

---

*Academic studies reveal conclusively that greed is a
fairly selfish thing.*

Professor Claudius Fritzenbacher III
Emeritus Professor,
Dept. of Verifiable Myths, Camford University.

Warm-ups
If you had to list your three major goals in life, what would
they be? How might you use money to help you achieve
each of these, without it becoming your master?

Study/Discussion
Look back over this chapter. What does the word
'materialism' mean? What do communism and capitalism
actually have in common? Discuss what you think are the
pros and cons of capitalism.

Describe each of the three kinds of poverty mentioned
in this chapter.

Read Deuteronomy 26:12; Psalm 72:1–4; Luke
14:12–14. What do you think these verses tell us about
God's attitude to poverty and the poor? (What about
Matthew 5:3?)

Read Matthew 6:25–33; Hebrews 13:20–21;
Deuteronomy 28:1–14. What do these verses tell you
about God's attitude to prosperity? Should Christians seek
poverty? Should they seek wealth?

Read 1 Timothy 6:17–19. What does God require of those who are already wealthy?

What do you think it means to live a life of 'limits'?

Getting Started
Draw up a simple, half-page budget based on what you currently spend each week. How can you adjust this to become more godly in your use of money?

Further Resources
Tom Sine, *Why Settle for More and Miss the Best?* (Word Books, 1989).

10

DID GOD HAVE A PREVIOUS LIFE?

– IS GOD A NEW AGER? –

Since childhood I have had memories of battlefields . . .
of men in steel fighting men in steel. Growing up
I simply accepted them. Now I know I was
remembering the clash between the Scots and the
English at the Battle of Flodden in 1513 . . . It
started at 4 p.m. and I was dead at about 5.15 p.m. . . .
I left five illegitimate children and a legitimate
17-month-old—who became James V.[1]

NO, THESE ARE NOT THE mutterings of someone on heavy medication! These are the serious musings of a respected playwright and author. She believes that in an exotic past life she was King James IV of Scotland. Once upon a time stories about people like this were found in little paperback books or comics in the 'Ghost Stories' section of the bookshop. Now you can find them in fairly respectable newspapers and magazines. Whole 'autobiographies' are written about past lives. People who've 'lived before' aren't thought of as freaks any more.

Why the interest in these stories? Perhaps it's because

people are looking for a way out of the humdrum of modern life. Or maybe it reflects the growing fascination with things esoteric and mysterious which has given rise to the popular movement we call the New Age.

What is this thing called the 'New Age'?

The New Age is different things to different people. To some, it represents a new business opportunity. There are great marketing opportunities here—there's a buck to be made. When people are tired of materialistic living and want to get in touch with their spiritual side—without doing any of the tough stuff which religious faiths like Christianity require of them—you can sell techniques which promise the world. People will part with cash for a little enlightenment in a flotation tank or through a regression therapy trip down 'memory lane'. All this is a variation of the old travelling medicine man, who hawked his bottles of coloured water from the back of a wagon.

For others, the New Age is the only possible saviour of the human race. We need to be rescued from our earth-destroying greed and mindless race for technological supremacy over each other. We need to get back to basics. We've just got to start thinking with the 'other' side of our brain, to abandon capitalistic competition and get some harmony, some 'convergence' happening between us. If we really work at it we can usher in a whole 'new age'. This is a variation on the 'make love, not war' and 'give peace a chance' catchwords of the sixties (with some 'Age of Aquarius' thrown in).

There are people who dabble 'around the edges' of

New Age ideas, taking what they think will suit their lifestyle and leaving the rest to the more devoted. Business people, housewives and husbands, university students, anyone looking for self-improvement or release from stress is a candidate here. Lifestyle magazines are filled with articles and adverts directed at these people. 'How to plot your moods by tracking the moon through the sky'; 'How to change your behaviour by painting your bedroom a different colour'; 'How to know you're sick by the lines on your eyes.' And so on . . .

To other people the whole thing is a 'load of bunk'. It's all mindless babble about things which don't matter by people who have nothing better to do with their time.

So why write a chapter on this phenomenon? Because the New Age represents more than a few colourful distractions for bored people. There's a system of thinking which runs all the way through it—right from the serious 'I've met with Martians' to the bedroom yoga practitioners. *And it's a dangerous pattern.*

Step one . . . Learn the language

Take a huge pot; throw in a strange mixture of Eastern and Western religious concepts; add some ideas on how to save the planet; put in some thoughts on do-it-yourself fitness and mental health, add a dash of 'how to reach your full potential', and there you have it—*the recipe for New Age soup!*

The New Age basically teaches that we are now at a turning point in history, an evolutionary breakthrough. A new world order is about to be ushered in—one in which peace and harmony hold everything together. We human beings are the ones who'll make all this possible. There's no need for belief in the Christian kind of God. Our problems have all been caused by the fact that we don't understand our infinite potential, we've lost sight of our own godhood.

To understand the New Age way of thinking, we have to learn some of the language. Here are a few of the key words, phrases and views:

Paradigm Shift . . . Sounds like the name of a space-age furniture removals company, but it's not. New Agers believe the human race can only be saved by finding a new way to think. We Westerners have forgotten how to think with the left side of our brain—the side neurologists say is for creative, abstract or lateral thinking. We're hooked on right-side thinking which means we're good at logic and mathematics. So we need a little help from the ancient East, where the most enlightened people were all good 'lefties'.

Higher Self . . . Human beings have largely forgotten that they not only got to where they are through evolution, but they're still evolving. Inside of us there is another waiting to get out, a self which is linked in with the 'Infinite Intelligence', the force holding the whole universe together. If we could just get in touch with the untapped power within us, if we could 'actuate our inner potential', then you'd see a change in the world, baby!

Transcendence, or Transformation . . . We've all got to learn to link up with one another, to think beyond our self, to see how interconnected we all are and to make it work for us. We've got to get our 'vibrations' right. If we can each tune our minds into the right universal wavelength, if we can all get our cells and molecules 'vibrating' together, we can free ourselves from our flaws and change the world in the process.

Gnosis . . . It's not who you know, it's what you know. There are age-old, mysterious pearls of spiritual wisdom we need to discover if we're going to get some transcendence happening. There are several planes of consciousness between where man is and where God is. Armed with the teachings of great gurus past and present, and disciplines like prayer, meditation and perhaps some magical rites thrown in, we can recover our lost divinity.

Mind . . . This means much more than the word 'brain' in normal English. It includes the brain, but it is also spiritual and is linked with the Higher Mind (the 'Force' of Star Wars fame) which pervades the universe.

Christ Consciousness . . . This is one of the dangers of New Age terminology—it sounds so deceptively like something else. It borrows terms from Christianity— and sometimes from science—to make itself sound more authoritative, more acceptable. What New Agers mean here is that we each have the potential to be a 'great man' like Jesus was, if we learn to play by their rules. Actually, the New Ager has a very different view of Jesus from the Bible, as we'll see.

Syncretism . . . The idea that, because all religions teach the same thing—that people are divine—we should be free to combine all their beliefs and practices under one big, rainbow-coloured umbrella!

Who invented the 'New Age' thing?

That's a bit like asking, 'Who designed greater Los Angeles?' I mean, there are some key contributors, but there are also many others who've just tacked on whatever they wanted, to wherever they wanted it. New Age is an eclectic religion—it borrows from many other sources. In some cases, that's embarrassing for New Age devotees, because they sometimes accept mutually exclusive ideas as all being true at once. Here are some of the key contributors to the great New Age sprawl:

Hinduism: People are born. They die. They're reborn. This continues until the person piles up enough good 'karma' to escape the life-death cycle. Good karma is earned through good works. You'll sweat it out doing good works for at least a few lifetimes before you achieve every person's great goal—godhood. This is a long way from Christian heaven! It means being united with the Universal Soul, being swallowed up in the force which keeps the universe going. It means losing your personal identity altogether.

There *is* no personal God in the Hindu scheme of things. You are as much a part of God as God is a part of you. Right and wrong are not absolutes, they're degrees on the same scale or line. There's no real difference between good and evil—they're relative terms.

And there is no one way to get to ultimate truth because all roads lead to heaven. According to Hindu thinking, it is impossible to say that a belief is either true or false—*everything goes,* everything! The key, they say, is tolerance. One Hindu puts it like this, 'Hinduism is a great storehouse of all kinds of religious experiments.'[2] In that respect, New Age borrows heavily from Hinduism.

An unfortunate by-product of reincarnation teaching, in the countries where it's been taught for centuries, is that

DID GOD HAVE A PREVIOUS LIFE?

it erodes people's desire to help others in need, or to change their world. If someone is poor, the thinking goes, it must because of bad karma from a past life—that person is getting no more than they deserve. To help them would be to upset the balance of things and to prevent them from doing what they need to do to improve their future lives! I agree with Richard Millikan, 'We lose an essential part of our glory when we relinquish the right to moral indignation.'[3]

Buddhism: This was born out of Hinduism. It is a form of philosophy first taught by a monk who lived in India 2,500 years ago. His name was Gautama Siddhartha, but he came to be known as Buddha, the 'Enlightened One'. *If* there is a God, say Buddhists, he is too big and complex for us to know, so there's not much we can say about God. A central idea of this religion is that 'mind' includes everything. You are one with the universe and everything in it.

Zen: There were books about this everywhere you looked in the sixties and seventies. They had titles like, *Zen and the Art of Motorcycle Maintenance* and *Zen and Cookery*. So, what is this religion which helps you in the garage and makes you a cullinary expert? It's a branch of Buddhism which teaches that enlightenment comes when we break off our commitments to logical, rational and material experiences.

Zen can be traced back to the Chinese religion of Taoism. The teaching is that behind the world we see there is the 'Tao', the eternal, unchanging 'principle' which holds it all together. The Tao keeps producing everything we see through the working together of two cosmic energy forces: the Yin and Yang. The Yin is female, passive and negative, the Yang is male, active and positive. Both are parts of the same thing, so good and evil are cut from the same cloth. There's good in all evil and evil in all good.

Mind over matter . . .

Gnosticism: First century gnostics believed that true wisdom is only available to certain elite people who have learned to think on a different level. The gnostics, of course, were those people! (Humble too!)

Ancient Greeks and Romans: Many of the rulers of these world kingdoms tried to mesh together all the religions of the countries they conquered, usually with themselves at the pinnacle.

Spiritualism: Around the turn of the century, people in the West started to take an interest in things Eastern, like religion. A host of new 'religions' were born around that time, which were based on taking ideas from the East and making them sound very Christian.

Mary Baker Eddy, the founder of Christian Science, taught that our problems exist only in our minds. We are as much a part of God as Jesus was, she said, so we should eliminate sickness by thinking it away! If we can just see our problems differently, they'll all blow away in the wind. This 'mind over matter' thinking is 'visualisation' techniques and is the basis of the modern fire-walking and spoon-bending pastimes.

Psychoanalysts: Sigmund Freud said that the human mind is driven by subconscious forces and instincts. Freud believed the most powerful of these was sexual in nature, but Carl Jung taught that a spiritual drive really made us tick. He said that there are a series of common thought patterns which are passed on from generation to generation. Many New Age channellers claim they're simply tapping into this 'universal consciousness', revealing great wisdom which is already deep within us.

Humanists: Abraham Maslow is the most famous of these. He told us that the greatest need human beings have is 'self-actualisation', the need to grow as a person. My inner nature is either good or neutral—*it is never bad.* Maslow's teachings are right smack at the centre of the modern Human Potential Movement. Listen to film stars and music idols these days. You'll hear so many talking about 'growing' as a person, or finding their 'true self' through their art. Maslow is trendy now.

What's the attraction?

'Lemon—The Ray of Cleansing: [Lemon] has no equal in the regeneration of an organism after debilitating illness . . . Main action is as a motor stimulant, cleansing to nervous tissue, encouraging the movement of deep congestion to the surface . . . Has some action as a bone and tissue builder, stimulating collagen manufacture, useful in removing scar tissue and abnormal growths . . .'[4]

All this from a colour?! Yep, *and more,* if you believe the magazines! The headline over this article was, 'Personal and Planetary Healing: Colour Ray Healing Chart.' Apparently colours can heal all manner of ills nowadays. Forget going to the doctor, call at the paint shop instead—it's cheaper. It may seem incredible to believe that people are buying into this kind of material. So what's the attraction of New Age techniques and teachings?

There are probably seven main reasons people get hooked on New Age thinking:

1. ***There's got to be more than what I see:*** In a recent hit single, megastar 'rocker' Sting sings, 'You could say I lost my faith in science and progress . . . ' Many people echo those sentiments.

The philosopher Nietsche said, 'God is dead and we have killed him.' Nietsche believed that the age of science would kill off humanity's need to believe in something 'out there', something or someone beyond itself. Yet, at the height of our love affair with technology, we find ourselves wanting reassurance that there's more to life than meets the eye. We're tired of living in a lonely, material universe—we're spiritual beings and we need to try to fill our thirst for reality on that deeper level. For some people New Age offers a chance to meet that need without giving up what they like about our self-centred capitalist ways.

History reveals that people become more inclined to reach out for spiritual truth whenever one millennium is about to end and another begins.

There were some real religious revivals towards the end of the last millennium, and the year 2000 will be, according to many New Agers, a key time in the dawning of a new era for humankind.

2. ***Institutional religion? It's lost in the fog:*** Sting again, 'You could say I lost my faith in the holy church.' Many people see historical Christianity only through the lens of their local newspaper—and the picture isn't a pretty one. It shows a group of people who don't believe any of the things they're supposed to, such as the Virgin Birth or the Resurrection of Jesus. And they fight among themselves so much! It seems like a dying dinosaur of an organisation, which is out of touch with the real world. New Age seems to some to offer a refreshing oppor-

tunity to have some kind of spiritual experience without taking on the excess baggage of dead ritual.

3. *I believe in everything, a little bit:* There's another reason people aren't committing themselves to traditional religious groups, they're finding commitment itself a tricky business. Since the seventies, marriage breakdown has tripled in many parts of the world. Some people are afraid to make long-term commitments either because they've been hurt before, or because they're not sure they have what it takes to keep their commitments. The New Age offers 'religious experiences' you can buy in a supermarket—you don't need to be committed to anything much except yourself. You don't even need to spend much time with other people if you don't want to.

4. *We've got to save the planet:* To some extent personal salvation has given way to planetary salvation. The pundits tell us that time is running out for our little habitat unless we each do something to save it. New Age offers all kinds of packages for involvement in saving the planet. Besides, personal salvation can be very uncomfortable—it means I have to deal with things 'in here', not just 'out there'.

5. *You can't tell me what to do:* Situation ethics— or 'do your own thing, but don't hurt anybody'—was popular in the fifties and sixties. Now it's the way of life. It's the popular myth of the day—and it is a myth—that you can have personal freedom without moral absolutes. With New Age there's no command to take up any crosses or make any stands you're not personally comfortable with—it's all options, and you can take them or leave them.

6. *I want to reach my full potential:* What's wrong with this one? Nothing, as long as self-interest is

your servant, not your master. For many people life consists almost totally of the quest for personal achievement and improvement. New Age can sound as if it's pressing all the right buttons when it comes to releasing 'the greatness within'.

7. *I can't see a thing!:* Why are so many people going for New Age material? Basically, because they're spiritually blind. The Bible tells us, 'The god of this age [Satan] has blinded the minds of unbelievers, so that they cannot see the light of the gospel of the glory of Christ, who is the image of God' (2 Corinthians 4:4). And there are none so blind as those who don't *want* to see.

But it's only a horoscope!

New Age thinking? No, I've got no time for that. What's that . . . my horoscope? . . . Sure, I read it now and again, for fun . . . What's astrology got to do with New Age?

Plenty. Of course, astrology was in vogue long before the term 'New Age' was even coined. The study of how the movements of the stars and planets might affect human destiny is as old as the tower of Babel (Genesis 11). Human beings are still trying to build their 'stairway to heaven', to play God, to know the future before it happens.

People are attracted to astrology for all kinds of reasons. Some people see it as harmless fun, a game that offers a little mystery and a few laughs. For some it's a money-making venture. It's not just about reading star-charts nowadays, there are all kinds of knick-knacks to be sold. For others, astrology is a way of gaining instruction about life without having to hear about morality. Then there are those for whom astrology has 'worked'—their astrologer has made some seemingly accurate pronouncements. Many of them come to see it as a religion, something to which you give your faith and trust your life.

Here's what former professional astrologer Charles Strohmer has to say on the subject, 'Even if your interest is superficial, perhaps you would think twice if you realised that when you turn to astrology you are actually turning to advice from the ancient gods of a peculiar polytheistic religion.'[5] This is the link between astrology and the New Age. They're both on about ancient religion. If you look into the texts used by astrologers, you'll find that what they interpret is not the planets but the gods those planets are named after.

'In the rationale of astrology,' says Strohmer, ' "gods" are assigned control over different parts of the human anatomy and over different spheres of human activity and personality. This should be clearly indicated throughout astrological literature. But it is concealed.'[6]

Astrologers are dishonest. They are not astronomers. They are not so concerned with star and planetary movements as they are with the way ancient mythological gods are supposed to pull the strings on human life.

It's all innocent fun, isn't it?

You will never read a newspaper horoscope which says: 'You, John Stephen Alexander Fritzenburger, will win the East-Doncaster under nineteen billiards championship at 7.30 p.m. today!'

Horoscopes written by people with unlikely names like 'Starwoman', are never very personal. (There are probably 60,000 other Librans out there reading that very same screed.) And they're not very specific either. The best they will do is say, 'You can expect a win today!', or, 'You can look forward to some good fortune.'

Sadly though, many people who've laughed at the 'harmless' horoscope in the paper will consult a personal astrologer when they get into some kind of trouble. That's the danger of magazine astrology—it can condition your thinking.

So what of this deeper level of astrology? Let's imagine a man goes to an astrologer for a personal consultation. We'll call the man Joe. By consulting charts and other astrological material, the astrologer comes up with a pretty accurate assessment of what Joe's like and a picture of his future which seems fairly reasonable.

The key to the astrologer's success in getting Joe to 'believe', is what is known in the star-reading trade as 'self-disclosures'. The experienced astrologer might look at Joe's star chart and manage to track down something very specific about him, some detail about a character trait, a past or present event, or some problem Joe's facing right now. Of course, the chart doesn't actually 'tell' the astrologer anything—it's how the chart is *interpreted* that matters—and that's a very subjective business.

What happens is that the astrologer gets a kind of hunch, an intuition, which he passes on to Joe. When the astrologer shares this with Joe, his jaw drops. 'How could he know that?' thinks Joe. ('How *did* I know that?' thinks the astrologer!)

After this, Joe is willing to trust the astrologer. He's open to accepting whatever the astrologer tells him about his future and he's also open to doing whatever he is told to do. What he is *not* aware of is that very often the amazingly accurate hunch which got him hooked was communicated by demonic spirits. The Bible calls them 'familiar' spirits—they know things about people because they are spiritual beings who can see into people's lives. (See Leviticus 19:31; Deuteronomy. 18:11; 1 Samuel 28:3.) Sometimes not even the astrologer is aware of the real source of the information.

The aim of these spiritual beings is to deceive Joe into believing and doing things which will ultimately result in his destruction—especially his spiritual destruction. They want him to be comfortable in his new-found beliefs, so that he never reaches out to God for help. Many times in the Bible we are warned not to associate with these powerful beings, because they will lead us into error and destruction, while promising so much more. (See Daniel 4:7; 5:7–8; Isaiah 47:13–14.)

A little bit of truth is used to draw Joe to a wrong conclusion. That's exactly the tactic Satan used to deceive Eve in Genesis chapter three. He hasn't changed tactics in a long time, because they work on so many people.

Astrology itself is based on ancient myths—not on truth—and there's a very real spiritual power lurking, waiting to exploit the hungry heart. It's a power the glossy magazines—and the astrologers—don't tell you about.

In my travels as a speaker over the years I've met people around the world who've been sent into confusion and despair because they've dabbled with what the Bible calls 'spiritual agents from the headquarters of evil'. (Ephesians 6:12, Amplified Version). Make no mistake, astrology *is* more than star-gazing! (And if you *are* a Christian, to dabble in horoscopes is to cut yourself off at the knees! See Mark 3:25–27.)

Former astrologer Strohmer has the final word, 'Because it is a counterfeit of authentic answers, it satisfies for a season—like counterfeit money does, until the counterfeiter is nabbed—but that's the best it can do. It must let you down. That is its nature—to tease; to tantalise, to parody.'[7]

Dancing with the devil . . .

Astrology is not the only aspect of New Age which flirts with occult forces. The word 'occult' means a form of 'knowledge' which is beyond normal human knowledge and is communicated only to the initiated, by supernatural spiritual forces. Most people know, though, that playing around with occult forces can get you badly burned. New Age has more to it than just health plans and personal development programmes. Here are a few areas in which it touches on the occult:

1. ***Wicca and Shamanism*** . . . Wicca is nature religion. It is another word for witchcraft. It's about worshipping 'created things rather than the Creator' (Romans 1:25). 'Shaman' is a fancy name for medicine man or witch doctor.

2. ***Second sight*** . . . This is the ability to see beyond our time frame, into the past, the future, or some 'other' present (also called clairvoyance). As with astrology, powerful demonic forces often bring people into bondage through this technique.

3. ***Divination*** . . . This is the gaining of knowledge through occult techniques such as reading tarot (or normal) cards, consulting the dead, or 'reading' the insides of chickens!

4. *Spirit guides* . . . These are your 'friendly neighbourhood spirits' who provide information through a medium, who has given complete control of him/herself to demonic forces. Jesus was in the business of putting demon spirits out of people's lives (Acts 10:38, Mark 1:26, Luke 4:33). The New Age tries to get them back in!

5. *Channelling* . . . A fancy word for demon possession. The Bible claims that mediums are right up there with people who sacrifice their children to 'fire gods' as far as God is concerned. Both activities are 'detestable' in His eyes (Deuteronomy 18:10–13). It's amazing how often channelled 'beings' talk about death being unreal; about the fact that we are all divine beings; and about salvation coming through tapping into the 'universal mind'. All these are the exact opposite of Bible teaching. (See Russell Chandler's *Understanding the New Age,* pp.80–88.)

6. *Astral projection* . . . The dangerous practice of going on temporary out-of-body joy-rides, in which there's precious little joy! Again, the overriding feature is the gradual loss of control over your life to outside spiritual forces.

7. *UFOs* . . . Have you met any little green men lately? Don't laugh, many people claim to have done just that. And it's often an occult-related experience, featuring visible manifestations of demonic spirits.

8. *Retrocognition* . . . Déjà-vu is a term used to describe the feeling—which we've all experienced—of having been somewhere before. Some people say this is evidence thatwe've all had past lives and been reincarnated. Retro-cognition is learning about past lives by use of the paranormal. Familiar spirits love to play this kind of game (and they always win)!

And the list goes on. (For more information on this, see *The New Age and You*, by Roger Ellis and Andrea Clarke, Kingsway, 1992.)

It's not what you know, but who you know that counts . . .

Hey, don't be fooled: New Age does clash with Christianity, and with a **Bang**!

New Age teaching is all about rebellion and deception. It's about rebellion because it puts 'me' and 'my potential' above God and His will. The Bible is clear—human beings are *not* God—they never have been and they never will be at any time now or in the future. Yes, we were created in God's likeness, but we were not made gods. We are not divine, we are human (Numbers 23:19; Isaiah 55:9). It's no accident that the Bible says, 'Rebellion is like the sin of divination' (1 Samuel 15:23), because both are based on taking short-cuts which leaves God out of the picture.

New Age is about deception, because 'evil' is not the same as 'good'. Evil is anything which is against the nature of God, anything which rebels against His right way of doing things. This is what the Bible calls sin (Isaiah 59:2; 43:24–25).

Yes, we are capable of doing good things, because even the worst person on earth still reflects something of the image of God. But, because of our moral Fall in the Garden of Eden, our basic inner bias is not towards good, but towards evil.

The Bible wants to help us wise up. We must not compromise with evil, it says, but overcome it with good (Romans 12:21). Satan's short-cut 'techniques' to higher, secret knowledge never work, and we should have learned that from the Garden of Eden. He's a liar and a cheat (Acts 13:8–12; 2 Corinthians 4:4; John 8:44). He sometimes comes 'masquerading as an angel of light' (2 Corinthians 11:14). He must be avoided at all costs (Luke 4:6–13; 1 Peter 5:8–9).

Christian writer and speaker John Stott put it this way:

> Human beings are capable of the loftiest nobility and the basest cruelty . . . Human beings are the inventors of churches for the worship of God, hospitals for the care of the sick, universities for the acquisition of wisdom. And human beings are also the inventors of torture chambers, concentration camps and nuclear arsenals. Strange paradox [this human being] . . . rational and irrational, moral and immoral, godlike and bestial.[8]

We might as well get used to the idea—we are not gods and we're not in a mess just because we forgot how to *be* gods! In fact, wanting to be 'like God' is the very thing which got us into this mess (see Genesis 3:5).

Our highest possible achievement could never be reaching godhood, it would mean to be the kind of human beings God intended us to be when He made us. But because we've got this inner evil bent to contend with, we can't even do that without God's help. We simply don't have what it takes to 'go it alone'.

Salvation for humankind will not come through getting our 'vibrations' right, or pulling together across the world like some great big happy family. It won't come through our talking to the dead or thinking nice thoughts. We won't be saved because we know how to sit in the lotus position and lose our worries in the 'great universal soul'. Salvation comes through us putting faith in the only one who saves—Jesus Christ (Acts 4:12).

On a Roman cross He did for us what we could never do for ourselves—He made our peace with God. He became our 'stand-in'; He took on Himself the pain we should suffer; He reaped what we had sown (Isaiah 53:4–6).

Hey, God Himself promised us a new age—the dawning of a new kingdom where lions and lambs would lie down together and the world would be at peace (Isaiah 11:1–11). But this would be a kingdom based on the lordship of His Son, not the self-mastery of human beings. We keep trying to find short-cuts to that kingdom; we keep trying to cut God out of His own picture. That's never worked. The Persians, Greeks and Romans in their turn all thought they had the right system for self-improvement. Where are their empires now?

It will only have its physical manifestation when Jesus returns (Revelation 11:15; 12:10). But before this happens men and women must be 'born into' this kingdom in a spiritual sense. We can't enter this kingdom until *it* enters *us,* until it begins to change us from the inside (John 3:3–5)! Through a personal relationship with Christ, and a total reliance on His power to save us, we throw open our lives to invasion by God's new kingdom.

You see, it's not *what* you know—what mystical knowledge you possess—it's *who* you know that counts. It's that simple, *and* that profound!

REFERENCES:

1. A. J. Stewart, quoted in 'I Died as I Led My Men into Battle', *Daily Mail* (27 June, 1994).
2. Quoted by Colin Chapman, *The Case For Christianity* (Lion Pub., 1981), p.146.
3. David Millikan and Nevill Drury, *World's Apart? Christianity and the New Age* (ABC Books, 1991), p.78.
4. *Australian WellBeing*, 1991 Annual, p.70.
5. Charles Strohmer, *What Your Horoscope Doesn't Tell You* (Word Books, 1991), p.15.
6. Ibid., p.17.
7. Ibid., p.129.
8. Quoted by Russell Chandler, *Understanding the New Age* (Word Books, 1989), p.305.

STUDY GUIDE

Biologists have discovered that there's more to our spirituality than meets the eye!

Professor Claudius Fritzenbacher III
Emeritus Professor,
Dept. of Verifiable Myths, Camford University.

Warm-ups
Can you describe a couple of ways in which New Age ideas have become part of our popular culture?

Study/Discussion
What are the major differences between New Age teachings and Christian belief?

Looking back over this chapter, what are the major problems with astrology, as far as a Christian is concerned? What does Mark 3:25–27 say about Christians who dabble in things like this?

Read Genesis 3:5; 2 Corinthians 4:4. What do you think these verses suggest about New Age teachings on 'the god within'? What does 2 Corinthians 11:14 suggest about the power behind New Age teachings?

Read Deuteronomy 18:10–13; Leviticus 19:31. What do these passages say about practices like 'channelling'?

Read Romans 1:25. How does this relate to practices such as 'Wicca' (nature religion)?

Getting Started
A friend of yours is into New Age ideas in a big way. What can you say to encourage your friend towards Christ?

Further Resources
Russell Chandler, *Understanding the New Age* (Word Books, 1989).
Charles Strohmer, *What Your Horoscope Doesn't Tell You* (Word Books, 1991).

11

CAN YOU PLAY GOD
(WITHOUT LOSING)?

– ABORTION AND HUMAN RIGHTS –

Foetuses about to be aborted should be anaesthetised before the operation in case they are capable of feeling pain, a doctor said today. A study in the Lancet *by a team of doctors and scientists reports that unborn babies may feel pain and might need anaesthetic or painkilling drugs before blood tests or transfusions.*[1]

ABORTION, EUGENICS AND euthanasia—these are considered to be among the most important human rights issues of our time. Ethicists, philosophers and theologians struggle to keep up with scientists as technology races ahead of our ability to set standards on how it should be used.

Rapid change is all around us, and progress will always demand change. But not all change is necessarily good. Some ethicists are worried that new technology is being used by interest groups to impose immoral ideas on the populace at large. George Grant, for example, gives us this warning, 'There is a force at work in our land . . . Not so much a grand conspiracy, but rather the practical outworking of social engineers who are, even at this moment, hard at work, having gained access to the highest offices of power in this land.'[2]

Whether you accept that kind of assessment or not, you've got to admit that the pace of technological change is bringing us face to face with some major moral questions. And it looks as if things will get even more confusing in the years ahead!

What do the words mean?

If you don't know how big an issue abortion is, you've been taking a very long holiday in another solar system! Hardly a week goes by without this issue—now also called 'termination of pregnancy'—appearing on our news-stands. But terms like 'eugenics' and 'euthanasia' are not yet as much in everyday usage.

Eugenics is the study of ways in which the physical and mental quality of a people can be controlled by genetic engineering. You'll remember that the Nazis did some of their most diabolical work in the 1930s when they tried, through sterilisation and other scientific means, to find ways of wiping out an entire race. Their justification for this was the basic philosophy behind eugenics—the improvement of the human race by selective breeding. When that didn't get quite the results they wanted they resorted to gas chambers.

Early supporters of eugenics were probably not think-ing along those lines, however. What they were trying to do, they said, was to improve the general intellectual qual-ity and behaviour of humanity by scientific means. They wanted to find ways to stop the spread of harmful genetic abnormalities which are passed on from one generation to the next.

Today, some Chinese provincial governments use eugenic principles by enforcing compulsory sterilisation on sections of the community. In 1986, Singapore adopted a policy through which women who were university graduates were guaranteed pay rises when they gave birth to a child. Women who had no tertiary qualifications were offered home grants when they gave birth, provided they were sterilised after the first or second child. Eugenics is alive and well.

You may not have heard much about eugenics, but you'll almost certainly be aware of euthanasia. Basically this is involves the so-called 'mercy killing' of someone with an incurable disease or illness. The Netherlands was the first nation to legalise it in 1983.

In America, though, the issue is still a real 'hot potato'. A doctor, whom some have called 'Doctor Death', fitted out a 'suicide van' in which a number of people with seemingly incurable conditions went to their deaths. It was basically a Volkswagen Kombi-van which contained a bed, an intravenous drip and a pump. When the 'patient' had climbed aboard, the doctor would insert the drip, then leave. The patient would then flick a switch and send a lethal dose of poison into their blood system.

Some legal authorities are not quite sure what to do with this doctor—lock him up or give him a medal. Perhaps they might read to him his Hippocratic Oath, which says, 'I will give no deadly drug if asked.'

Abortion—playing God or the compassionate choice?

It would take volumes to deal with all three of the issues mentioned above, and others have done a great job of it. So I want to restrict my comments here to abortion in particular, for two simple reasons.

First of all, because it's the human rights issue which affects most people in our world today (it affects a whole lot more if you include the unborn). And secondly, because your response to abortion is pretty much a litmus test for how you'll feel about the other issues. The principles and processes we use to arrive at our moral judgements will be consistent across the board. If we can justify abortion, we can probably justify the other two. If we think abortion is 'not on', then we'll tend to vote conservatively on eugenics and euthanasia.

So, what's all the fuss about? Abortion is a surgical procedure which has only recently been legalised in most developed countries. Illegal and dangerous abortions have been carried out for hundreds, perhaps thousands of years. And of course the terminating of a pregnancy when the mother's life is in danger is nothing new.

But abortion on demand—where there are no other issues than a woman's choice involved—is something new. It wasn't allowed in most developed countries until the late sixties and early seventies. At the forefront of the push for abortion on demand were the radical feminist movements which claimed that this was an issue of women's rights.

Following the weakening of anti-abortion laws, the number of abortions performed jumped dramatically in many countries. Japan broke its ban on abortion in 1948 and a staggering five million abortions were performed in the first eight years after that. In the USA, a legal case called *Roe vs. Wade* led to the supreme court calling the Texas anti-abortion laws 'unconstitutional'. The door was thrown open for new pro-abortion laws.

In 1969 there were less than 20,000 abortions performed in America; during the eighties, there had been more than 1.5 million! In Washington DC, the nation's capital, abortion is said to outnumber live births by three to one![3]

Who Cares?

The abortion issue is an important one to several major groups of people:

1. *Women who don't want a baby:* There are many reasons why a woman might not want a baby, and they're not all completely selfish. For example, a family might already be too big for the budget to cope with and having another mouth to feed won't help matters. Or the father might be a brute who bashes his children mercilessly.

Some women feel emotionally ill-equipped to raise a child and don't want to do a bad job of it. Others have been the victims of sexual assault or incest and feel they could not love a child conceived in such horrific circumstances. There also are some who suffer from hereditary diseases and have good reason to believe their child would inherit them.

We'll take another look at this issue in a moment.

2. *Radical women's rights movements:* These are groups which have been formed to influence governments and change attitudes in the community towards the

needs of women. Unfortunately, they've often shut many women out of the work they're doing, by becoming voices for lesbianism and other radical fringe interests.

The radical women's movement calls abortion an issue of women's rights—the human embryo is growing in a woman's body and is thus her 'property'. She has the right to do whatever she likes with it. These groups use issues like abortion to stir up emotion in favour of their underlying, and often hidden, agendas. They've used abortion to divide people into two groups which suit their cause—those who are 'for' women's rights and those who are 'against'. If you say abortion on demand is wrong, you're anti-woman!

When a group of people use an issue as a political tool, they tend to bend the truth from time to time in order to score political points. Pro-abortionists certainly have their share of political dirty tricks up their sleeves. I read one pamphlet which told teenage girls that 'abortion is the safest surgical procedure in the world' and that it was 'safer than having your tonsils out'![4]

3. **Medical researchers:** Imagine this. You're lying on a table with medical instruments all around you. There's a bright light in your eyes and several instruments attached to your bald head. You're about to have a brain transplant!

Impossible? No, it's happening right now! Science isn't quite at the stage where it can rip out your used cortex and replace it with a brand-new model, but doctors have already begun operations in which cells from aborted foetuses are used to heal human brains.

In 1989, a Swedish team took brain cells, taken from several aborted foetuses and inserted them into a faulty part of a grown man's brain. The man had been suffering from a Parkinson's-like disease brought on by taking a bad batch of 'designer' drugs. A couple of years later the man had made an almost complete recovery from his paralysing condition. The 'harvested' cells had done just about all that was asked of them, producing important chemicals which the man's brain had stopped making.[5]

Researchers are hopeful that they'll soon be able to use foetal cells in all kinds of studies and operations. But there are many voices of concern—experts are worried about the abuse of this kind of power. Some have asked, 'What's to stop the forming of "abortion industries", which pay women in poor countries to conceive so that their foetuses can be removed for experimentation?' Others have wondered, 'If we now accept experimentation on unborn people, what will stop scientists later from wanting to experiment on people who are comatose, or dying'? And what's to stop the use of aborted cells in eugenics-type experiments like the ones the Nazis carried out?

One point cries out to be made—*there are far more abortions carried out right now than could ever be justified on the basis of scientific research.*

Abortion is one of those issues which doesn't seem to have any middle ground—you're either very much in favour or very much against. It has become big business for some, and for others it's big-time politics. The pro-abortion lobby groups see it all as an issue of rights. The anti-abortionists believe they are defending the defenceless, the unborn. Which is right? Is there a right and wrong in issues like this? If so, how do we find the right path?

How is it done?

Before we look at the 'why' or 'why not' of abortion we should consider the methods which are used. There are four:

1. ***Dilation and curettage:*** The cervix is dilated so that a curette can be inserted. This is used to scrape the walls of the womb, tearing the foetus apart. The pieces of the foetus are then removed by suction through a tube.

2. ***Injection of toxic solution:*** A long needle is used to inject a solution—usually saline—which poisons the sac surrounding the foetus, burning and killing the foetus.

3. ***Surgery:*** Procedures similar to a Caesarian section are used when the abortion is performed late in a pregnancy. The difference is the baby is taken to be 'terminated', not saved.

4. ***Abortion Pill:*** The French pill RU 486 was released on the market in several countries a few years back. It's also called the 'morning after' pill, because it brings on a chemical reaction in the womb which causes the egg to be rejected. It can cause heavy bleeding and is only about 80 per cent effective.

The big questions . . .

OK, so why is abortion right, or why is it wrong? Is it an evil abuse of human freedoms or a necessary part of complex life in modern times? To answer these questions we must first answer a few others. The first is, 'What are the truly fundamental human rights and where did we get them from?'

Many countries have statements about human rights

embedded in their constitutions. America and France formulated their first statements on human rights as a result of their respective revolutions. Even earlier in history, in the year 1215, England's King John reluctantly introduced the Magna Carta. This document basically protected common people from the abuse of royal powers. It set up, among other things, the 'trial by a jury of peers' system of justice. Later on, the British Bill of Rights (1688–9) made the monarch subject to the parliament to further protect the interests of the people.

Of course there are often disagreements between various countries when it comes to human rights. But, generally speaking, most nations and cultures across the world share fairly common views on human rights.

The United Nations Commission on Human Rights receives approximately 20,000 complaints every year. They range from accusations against governments for the ill-treatment of political dissidents, to charges against police forces for improper interrogation techniques, to accusations of prejudice against minority groups. This Commission couldn't exist if many different nations of the world couldn't agree on certain basic standards for how human beings should be treated.

Where does this underlying sense of right and wrong come from?

In 1791 Thomas Paine published one of the first books on human rights, called simply *The Rights of Man*. Paine was a deist—he believed in the existence of some kind of God simply because his reason told him there must be one. He didn't believe, as Christians do, that God gives personal revelation to human beings and wants relationship with them. Just by looking at the evidence before him, in nature and history, Paine came to believe that human rights weren't something we invented for ourselves. Our rights, said Paine, were given to us way back at the time of our creation. They are bequests from our Maker. Thomas Jefferson echoed this when he wrote that 'all men are created equal' and that they are 'endowed by their Creator with certain inalienable rights'.

Now if God gave us our rights, two things are true. First of all nobody can take those rights away; no one has the right to say, 'OK, that's enough of that, you don't have those rights any more!' Secondly, every one of us will answer not just to humankind, but to God for the way we treat other members of our race.

So, what are our rights? Thomas Jefferson wrote about the rights to, 'life, liberty and the pursuit of happiness'. In 1941 President Roosevelt spoke about four major human rights—freedom of speech, freedom to worship, freedom from want and freedom from fear. But if God gave us our rights, what does *He* have to say about them?

Human rights, God's way

According to the Bible, when God made us He gave us three things in particular. The first was dignity. John Stott shows how Genesis 1:27–28 describes this dignity in several ways.[6] First of all, human beings are made in God's image, which means we have dignity because of our relationship to Him. We're not the same as the animals, we're unique.

Secondly, human beings come in two basic 'packages'—male and female—and we have dignity in the special relationship we enjoy with each other. Animals don't marry—at least, they don't where I come from! Thirdly, human beings were told to rule over—not abuse—the world they lived in. We have dignity because we are God's chosen stewards of His creation. All human beings have the right to be treated with proper respect, simply because they are human!

The second thing God gave us was equality. The Bible is clear that no powerful person or group should impose their will on the weak. Proverbs 14:31 tells us, 'He who oppresses the poor shows contempt for their Maker, but whoever is kind to the needy honours God.' All human beings have the right to be treated equally. None should be discriminated against on the basis of their physical condition, age, sex, race, material wealth or position in society.

The third of God's gifts to us was responsibility. As Stott puts it, 'The Bible says much about defending other people's rights, but little about defending our own . . . It emphasises that our responsibility is to secure the other person's rights. We must even forgo our own rights in order to do so.'[7]

The Bible says more about responsibilities than it does about rights. Jesus taught that my first responsibility is to love God with everything I've got, the second is to love my neighbour as myself (Matthew 22:37–40). The Old Testament prophet Micah said the same thing in a different way, 'He has showed you, O man, what is good. And what does the Lord require of you? To act justly and to love mercy and to walk humbly with your God' (Micah 6:8).

As human beings, then, we have the right to be

respected whatever our circumstances. We have the right to be treated fairly and without prejudice. And we have the responsibility to fight for the rights of other people (and God!). All of our behaviour, says Stott, should be 'compatible with the humanness God created and intends to safeguard'.[8]

When is a human not a human?

OK, so God gave us our rights. In relation to the abortion question we now have another question to answer. Is an embryo or foetus human? ('Embryo' describes the new life up until two months after conception; 'foetus' describes it after that time.) Is it just a bundle of cells or does it have human status—and therefore human rights?

People have basically five views on when the embryo becomes human. *You must make your choice from these options.*

1. You might choose to believe that the embryo or foetus is just a piece of tissue, a growth on the mother's womb, which she can have removed if she likes.

2. Your second option is that the embryo or foetus becomes human somewhere between conception and birth. This one is tricky.

3. Or you might decide that the embryo becomes a person only after it reaches what is called 'viability', the time when the foetus can survive on its own.

4. You can see birth itself as the crucial moment when 'personhood' begins.

5. Finally, you might conclude that the embryo has been human all along, right from the time it was first conceived. If that's the case, the embryo has had rights from the very beginning, and you and I have no right to tamper with it unnecessarily! This is the option supported by the Bible, and it's not as crazy as some people will tell you.

In Bible terms the embryo is like the seed of a tree—*it isn't yet all that it will become, but it contains everything needed to get there!* Within the embryo are all the mechanisms which will one day form an adult human being. It's not a 'potential' human being—it *is* human.

But there's even more to it than that. The Bible says that we should treat the embryo as a person because it is known and loved by God. In His eyes an embryo isn't an animal, or a lump of jelly—an embryo is a human being for whom He has very special plans. Jesus was very clear on the fact that every person has great value in this world—not because of their achievements or status, but *primarily* because they are prized by God (Luke 12:24).

Jeremiah was a young man when God called him to be a prophet to his people. Feeling a little self-conscious, Jeremiah wondered if he could make it in that role. God gave him this encouragement, 'Before I formed you in the womb I knew you, before you were born I set you apart; I appointed you as a prophet to the nations' (Jeremiah 1:5).

Later in the Bible, Paul encouraged the Ephesian Christians with these words, 'For he [God] chose us in him [Christ] before the creation of the world to be holy and blameless in his sight. In love he predestined us to be adopted as his sons through Jesus Christ . . . ' (Ephesians 1:4–5). Then he told his young friend Timothy, 'This grace [which saves us] was given us in Christ Jesus before the beginning of time' (2 Timothy 1:9). What does all this mean? That God knew our individual potential *before time began* and even then intended us to enjoy the best He had to offer.

There are a number of other places where the Bible talks about the destiny of unborn children. Before conception had even taken place, God's angel told Samson's parents about how they should raise their special son (Judges 13:6–14). A similar angel visited Zechariah to prophesy what kind of boy his son John the Baptist would become—before his wife had conceived (Luke 1:11–24).

An angelic messenger also told Mary all about the baby she would bring into this world. Again, this was before she even became pregnant (Luke 1:34). After Mary had conceived, God instructed Joseph not to worry about her being a virgin, and explained again how special this child would be and what he would do (Matthew 1:20–21). Now if all this was happening today, some people might be counselling Mary to have an abortion. Where would history be then?

Hey, if a baby is valuable to God *before it is even conceived*—because *He* knows what it will grow to become—how can it be of less value afterwards? I love the way the writer of Psalm 139 talks about the unborn:

> For you created my inmost being;
> > you knit me together in my mother's womb.
> I praise you because I am fearfully
> > and wonderfully made;
> > your works are wonderful,
> > I know that full well.
> My frame was not hidden from you
> > when I was made in the secret place.
> When I was woven together in the
> > depths of the earth,

> your eyes saw my unformed body.
> All the days ordained for me
> were written in your book
> before one of them came to be.
>
> (Psalm 139:13–16)

When is an embryo human? The Bible's answer is: *right from the start!*

Where do morals come from?

Everybody recognises the importance of living to a system of values, having some sort of moral code. Morals are simply standards of right and wrong. They're more than laws, because no matter how laws change, conscience can still prick the emotions about the way we ought to behave. We usually expect our politicians to live morally. Most of us want to work for a boss who behaves morally. We certainly want our husbands and wives to live by a moral code, not to mention our children.

For all of our talk about 'doing your own thing', there's a sense of crisis today in relation to public morality. People are concerned about rising crime rates and family breakdown. Voters are frustrated and angered by the lack of scruples shown by leaders in public office. Juvenile delinquency is on the increase in many Western nations and class warfare has broken out because of oppression and greed. More than ever we need a set of moral values which are generally shared and honoured throughout the community.

That's what we all want, but morality like this doesn't come cheaply! We need morality that's based on more than our fickle human tastes. Public opinion changes too quickly, and is too motivated by selfishness for us to base our sense of right and wrong on that.

We need value systems which are built on absolutes. Absolutes are universal laws, descriptions of how things always are, no matter who's in power, or what is the fashion of the day. Is it ever right to murder someone in cold blood? No. Is it ever right to steal someone else's property? No. Oh, you can come up with all the fancy-sounding rationalisations you like to avoid absolutes, but at some point in your life you'll want to fall back on them! (If someone's about to murder you, you're not going to be saying, 'Sure, murder's OK; go for it if it turns you on!')

Moral absolutes are 'absolute'—unchanging and all-encompassing—because they're based on the greatest Absolute of all, the moral character of an unchanging God. All of God's creation reflects His nature. To live in a way which is inconsistent with God's character, to deny the absolutes in His universe, is to work against the very fabric which holds the whole thing together.

As you can imagine, summing up the nature of God in a few paragraphs is impossible. In fact, you couldn't do it with all the words in all the books in all the world. But according to the Bible there are at least two fundamental things we can say about the nature of our Maker. Both of these have something to say on the issue of abortion.

The first thing we need to know about God is that He is just. He's scrupulously fair in everything He does. Actually, it's true to say that God doesn't just *act* justly, He *is* justice itself. What we call justice is simply a reflection of God's character. And He has built that 'justice-factor' into His natural creation. You will always reap what you sow—

if you put apple seeds in the ground you'll get an apple tree. If you lie your way through a relationship, your lies will someday, some way, work against you. You can't escape it—what goes around comes around.

That's very good news when you think about it. I mean, who'd want to live in a universe where the Hitlers, Stalins and Ceausescus went unpunished for their inhumanity. The God of the Bible has promised them—and those they persecuted—justice, if not in this life then certainly in the hereafter!

The Judaeo-Christian concept of justice is based on the legal and prophetic writings of the Old Testament. It has stood societies in great stead for millennia. One of the very foundations of that justice system is the idea that the poor, the weak and the unprotected should be given a 'fair go' in law.

Jesus understood and defended the basics of Old Testament law—like the Ten Commandments—more than any man had done before. He knew that the 'thou-shalt's' and 'thou-shalt-not's' were absolutes, which reflected the justice of God. He certainly taught compassion for the poor and that both good and evil deeds would have their reward. As one writer puts it, Christianity teaches that, 'A society's maturity and humanity will be measured by the degree of dignity it affords to the disaffected and the powerless.'[9]

God's justice must be brought into any discussion on an issue like abortion. As we've already seen, the unborn are human beings in God's eyes. If that's true, and God demands that we take special care of the defenceless, what can we say except that those who end these young lives for no good reason will answer for their injustice?

The other characteristic of God's nature which we need to consider here is His love. God doesn't just *feel* love, or even *decide* to love, He *is* love. What is it that stops the Ten Commandments, and the rest of the Bible's laws, from being arbitrary lists of dos and don'ts? The love of God.

Jesus despised the way some religious authorities imposed laws without compassion. The Pharisees of his day knew what the law of God said, but their application of it always lacked compassion and mercy. They became nit-picking 'pains in the neck' because they took God's nature out of God's law—and that's just about as counter-productive as having no law at all!

The Pharisees saw God only as a judge, a disciplinarian. In contrast, Jesus' favourite word for God was 'Father'. According to Jesus, God's greatest act in human history was one of love (John 3:16). Justice was involved too—I deserved the eternal death which was coming to me (Romans 3:23; 6:23). But God in His love for me allowed Jesus to take that punishment, to become my 'Fall Guy'. Thus God's love fulfilled all that God's justice required, but at the greatest possible cost to Him!

Love is an absolute which must also be brought into our discussion about abortion. Love will cause us to empathise with those women who do not feel able to handle motherhood, but instead of killing their unborn child—which would offend God's justice—we should find ways to support them in their motherhood, or to help them have their child adopted.

Where a woman is pregnant due to rape or incest, justice again will rule out abortion. But love will demand that those around her offer support and healing for her shattered self-esteem and her understandable sense of violation and outrage.

What about where genetic abnormalities are expected to show up in the new baby? Imagine you've heard that a baby was about to be born whose mother has tuberculosis and whose father has syphilis. There are four other children in the family: one was born blind, the second died, the third is deaf and dumb and the fourth has tuberculosis. Knowing all that, would you end the pregnancy? If your answer is 'yes', congratulations, you've just killed Beethoven!

But what if all the scans show that a child will definitely be born deformed? Wouldn't it be better for the child if he or she doesn't have to go through life carrying that load? To say that physically or mentally disabled people can't enjoy a rich and full life is to play God. What we're really asking is, 'Wouldn't it be easier for us if we didn't have them?'

So many people who have disabilities lead full and very productive lives, serving others with distinction and making a great contribution to this world. Young Stephen Wiltshire has an extraordinary talent for sketching. He is a shy genius whose drawings have won international acclaim. He's also a very gifted musician. TV shows have been made about him and he's travelled the world with his art. Yet he suffers from autism, which means that he has not developed normally in language or social behaviour. Sometimes he seems to just 'shut off' to the world around him and shrink back into his own private universe.

Do we have the right to say that someone like Stephen has no chance of leading a meaningful and rich life?

Or do we kill people who go through tragic accidents which leave them paralysed? No, because that would be neither just nor loving. Besides, science is constantly coming up with new ways to alleviate suffering and bring 'normality' to these people. So why treat the unborn disabled any differently?

It's not really too surprising that in the battered heartland of what used to be the Soviet empire, Russia, most women have between four and five abortions in a lifetime.[10] That reflects a system of government which denied God, and ruled out His justice and love as foundations for human behaviour. It also demeaned humanity in the process.

Help me if you can . . .

As you read this you may know someone who needs help in dealing with an unwanted pregnancy. Or you may be wrestling with the abortion question in your own situation. You or your friend need to do three things:

1. *Think for yourself:* Don't be a victim of conformity. Pro-abortionists like to talk about freedom of choice, but they rarely tell the whole truth about the aftereffects of abortion.

The physical complications can include damage to the cervix, puncturing of the uterine wall and infection of the Fallopian tubes. Also, the emotional loss and grief can take years to come to terms with. After one of my seminars for parents, a woman came up to me in tears. She had a lovely little girl at her side. I asked if there was something I could do to help her.

'No, I'm OK,' she responded. 'It's just that, well, God loves me so much—He gave His Son for me. And I killed mine! I had an abortion a few years back. Please pray that I'll be able to get through the grief I still feel.' (Note: I had hardly mentioned abortion that night, so I wasn't laying any 'guilt trips' on her!)

2. ***Think beyond yourself:*** Remember that your rights aren't the only ones. Others have rights—including the unborn. The life inside a pregnant woman is a human life. It's not an animal, or a piece of tissue.

Even if you don't accept what the Bible says about the unborn, check out the work of photographers like Lennart Nilsson, who published amazing photographs of babies at different stages of their development in their mothers' wombs. (See *Life* magazine, August 1990.) After just six weeks the photographs show the baby's arms and legs starting to take shape. After seven weeks the eyes have formed and the brain is visible above them. Yet most abortions, in Britain for example, are carried out on foetuses aged under twelve weeks![11]

Reread the quote at the beginning of this chapter. Science itself isn't totally convinced that unborn children don't suffer during abortions!

3. ***Seek out networks of support:*** Hunt down friends who will offer more than just clichéd answers. When people advise you to have an abortion it is often because they can't—or don't want to—offer any ongoing practical support when your baby is born.

Childbirth is a gift from God—a painful one to be sure, but precious all the same. It can be enjoyed rather than endured if you place God's love at the centre of your own life. There are some brilliant church and community groups around who are dedicated to helping young mothers (and fathers) raise their children well.

4. ***Take the long view:*** How do you want history to remember you? What kind of world do you want to pass on to your children?

Today, Christians in particular should work to save the unborn. But not by blowing up clinics and shooting abortionists—these are both unjust and unloving responses to the issues. We should be a prophetic voice, speaking out against injustice and preaching absolutes, but also mixing our morality with mercy.

Is it possible that one day, in a few hundred years from now, people will look back and thank God that humanity gave up on abortion, just as it did on slavery? Is it possible that at the forefront of that change were Christians who lovingly, wisely and courageously put their case, as did abolitionists like Wilberforce centuries before? We should all hope so!

REFERENCES:

1. 'Foetuses May Feel Pain, Say Doctors', *The Guardian* (8 July, 1994).
2. George Grant, *The Family Under Seige* (Bethany House Pub., 1994), p.23.
3. John Stott, *Issues Facing Christians Today* (Marshall Pickering, 1984), p.310.
4. See Mal Fletcher, *Youth: The Endangered Species* (Word Books, 1993), p.75.
5. *Brain Transplant*, American PBS TV, 1994.
6. Stott, op. cit., pp.154–156.
7. Ibid., pp.159, 160.
8. Ibid., p.156.
9. Paul Oestreicher, quoted by Stott, op. cit., p.157.
10. *The World At Noon*, ABC-TV, (9 September, 1994).
11. *The Guardian*, ibid.

STUDY GUIDE

*University studies have shown that if God could be
expressed in a mathematical formula, it would be a
seriously long one!*

Professor Claudius Fritzenbacher III
Emeritus Professor,
Dept. of Verifiable Myths, Camford University.

Warm-ups

What do you think is meant by the term 'human rights'?
List two or three things which you think are rights for all
human beings.

Study/Discussion

Read Matthew 22:37–40; Micah 6:8. What do you think
these passages tell us about human rights?

Read Jeremiah 1:5; Judges 13:6–14; Luke 1:11–24;
Matthew 1:20–21. What do these passages suggest about
how God sees abortion?

John Stott has said that, 'A society's maturity and
humanity will be measured by the degree of dignity it
affords to the disaffected and the powerless.' Discuss this
statement in the light of abortion and euthanasia.

Read Psalm 139:13–16 and put your name in every
time it says 'I'.

Getting Started

A young woman says she is pregnant but doesn't want a

baby. She is thinking of having an abortion. What can you say and do for her which might convince her to have her child?

Further Resources
John Stott, *Issues Facing Christians Today* (Marshall Pickering, 1984).

OK, SO HOW DO I BECOME A CHRISTIAN?

After reading this book or taking part in discussions with friends, you may be ready now to commit your life into God's hands, and find His total plan for you as an individual. Here's how to start:

1. Admit that you need help from above, that you are a part of God's fallen world in need of salvation (Romans 3:23).

2. Admit that only Jesus, the holy Son of God, could save you—that none of your good works is enough to do it! (Ephesians 2:8–9)

3. Confess, in prayer to God, that when Jesus died He did it for you, to make you right with God again. Tell God that you accept His gift of salvation through Jesus (Matthew 20:28).

4. Ask God to forgive all your failings and to make you pure within (1 John 1:9).

5. Thank God that Jesus' tomb is now empty—He did rise from the dead! This is a sign that God accepted His sacrifice on your behalf and that Jesus *is* trustworthy, so He *will* keep His promises to you (John 11:25).

6. Commit yourself to finding God's plan for your life and fulfilling it, leaving old, harmful habits behind (Galatians 2:20; Ephesians 2:10).

7. Live life to the maximum, in Jesus' power! (2 Corinthians 5:17).

Well, now we're family, you and I. So, see you in heaven, if not before!

Mal Fletcher

MAJOR REFERENCES
USED IN THIS BOOK

Campolo, Anthony, *Partly Right*, Word Books, 1985.

Campolo, Tony, *How to Rescue the Earth Without Worshipping Nature*, Word Books, 1992.

Chandler, Russell, *Understanding the New Age*, Word Books, 1989.

Chapman, Colin, *The Case for Christianity*, Lion Publishing, 1981.

Cooke, Kaz, *Real Gorgeous*, Allen and Unwin, 1994.

Cunningham, Loren, *Daring to Live on the Edge*, YWAM Pub., 1991.

Barna, George, *The Frog in the Kettle*, Regal Books, 1990.

Ellis, Roger and Clarke, Andrea, *The New Age and You*, Kingsway, 1992.

Ellul, Jacques, *The Presence of the Kingdom*, Helmers and Howard, 1989,

Fletcher, *Mal, Youth: The Endangered Species*, Word Books, 1993.

Grant, George, *The Family Under Seige*, Bethany House Publishers, 1994.

Hutchinson Softback Encyclopedia, Random Century Group, 1991.

Dennis, T. Lane, *The Letters of Francis Schaeffer*, Kingsway, 1985.

Martin, Joan, *The Ladies Aren't for Silence*, Word Books, 1991.

McDowell, Josh, *Evidence that Demands a Verdict*, Here's Life Publishers, 1979.

McMillen, Dr S. I., *None of These Diseases*, Spire Books, 1979.

Millikan, David and Drury, Nevill, *Worlds Apart? Christianity and the New Age*, ABC Books, 1991.

Peters, Tom, *The Tom Peters Seminar*, MacMillan, London, 1994.

Reisman, Eichel, Court, Muir, *Kinsey, Sex and Fraud: The Indoctrination of a People*, Huntington House Publishers, 1990.

Sehnert, Keith, W., MD, *Selfcare, Wellcare*, Augsburg Publishing House, 1985.

Sherman and Hendricks, *Your Work Matters to God*, NavPress, 1987.

Sine, Tom, *Why Settle for More and Miss the Best?*, Word Books, 1989.

Sine, Tom, *Wild Hope*, Monarch, 1991.

Stewart van Leeuwen, *Marty, Gender and Grace: Women and Men in a Changing World*, Inter-Varsity Press, 1990.

Stott, John, *Issues Facing Christians Today*, Marshall Pickering, 1984.

Strohmer, Charles, *What Your Horoscope Doesn't Tell You*, Word Books, 1991.

Toffler, Alvin, *Future Shock*, Pan Books, 1971.